OP 1st 10ᵘ

SEA BAG
OF MEMORIES

SEA BAG
OF MEMORIES

Images Poems Thoughts and Crafts
Of The Small Ship Sailors of
World War II

by

Wm. J. Veigele

Sea Bag of Memories
Images Poems Thoughts and Crafts
of The Small Ship Sailors of World War II

by

Wm. J. Veigele

Published by
Astral Publishing Co.
P. O. Box 3955
Santa Barbara, CA 93130-3955

www.astralpublishing.com

Cloth — First Edition — 2003

Copyright © 2002 by Wm. J. Veigele

Library of Congress Cataloging in Publication Data
Wm. J. Veigele
Sea Bag of Memories: cloth, 320 pages, notes, index

1.World War II, 2.Navy, 3. Coast Guard 4.Patrol Craft, 5.Subchasers, 6.Minesweepers, 7.Gunboats, 8.Cutters, 9.Nonfiction, 10.Poetry, 11.Handcrafts, 12.Drawings, 13.Paintings, 14. Cartoons, 15.Engineering plans, 16.Ship models

Library of Congress Control Number: 2001130579

ISBN: 0-9645867-4-6

Printed in the United States of America

I dedicate this book to all the young men who served on the small submarine chasers, patrol craft, minesweepers, gunboats, Cutters, and other small combat ships of the United States Navy and Coast Guard during World War II.

ACKNOWLEDGMENTS

First and foremost I thank my wife, Sue, for her generous help and steadfast encouragement while I was writing this book.

Many persons contributed material for use in this book. Their contributions were of equal importance and interest, so, not to suggest favoritism, I list here the contributors in alphabetical order by last name.

George Amaral, Al Angelini, Robert Baldwin, Carter Barber, Lee Barber, Christian Beilstein, Al C. Bellanca, Conrad Brown, William Buffington, Harry Burry, James H. Byington, Jr., Todd Cabral, Warren A. Cabral, Edward J. Comeau, Bob Crowl, Clyde Dauben, Melvin DeWitt, Jim Dickie, Phil Donahue, Richard K. Elmendorf, H. Finneran, Sid Frey, Ray Goin, Page G. Harman, Donald R. Hatfield, Norm Helford, Orris Hicks, Joseph G. Hoff, Jack Hogan, Kenneth A. Hooks, Gary W. Johnson, Wesley G. Johnson, Herbert Katzenberg, Joseph Kelliher, James F. Kennedy, Tom Kermen, Alex Kilpatrick, Bill Kinney, Robert S. Laurie, Bill Layton, Michel Lelievre, Peter Lessing, Darius Lipinski, Joe Luca, Nora McCarthy, Darrell McClure, James McMahon, Andrej Mista, Oris E. Moore, William Moore, James F. Morgan, Elmer G.

Muth, Wilbur F. Otto, Raymond Page, Jack M. Passmann, Marvin D. Polin, Tom A. Pollock, W. J. Rawlins, Tony Rego, Elra J. Reitz, Michael Reitz, Rick Reynolds, Robert B. Rice, Doug Roberts, R. H. Rushing, Thomas R. Sargent, K. J. Schwartz, Ed E. Sidebottom, Dick Sloane, Frank G. Soulier, Douglas P. Spade, John B. Tombaugh, William Tormey, Donald F. Townsend, Theodore R. Treadwell, Charles P. Turner, Jacob VanBelkum, Hugh Webster.

Personnel from various organizations also sent me material that I used in this book. These organizations are listed in the next paragraph.

Institute for Great Lakes Research; Linda Wheeler of the Hoover Institution Library at Stanford University; Patrol Craft Sailors Association; Bay County Historical Society, Jennifer Harbster of the United States Library of Congress; United States Navy Bureau of Ships; United States Navy Historical Center.

I also express my special thanks to James Hiney for modeling the sailor in the picture on the dust jacket and to Dr. Dan Caldwell for the photograph used as background on the dust jacket.

NOTE TO THE READER

Numbers that appear as superscripts in the text refer to additional information given in the Section titled Notes.

TABLE OF CONTENTS

Thousands of their soldiers
Looked down from their decks and
laughed,
Thousands of their sailors
Made mock of the mad little craft.

From "The Revenge: A Ballad of the Fleet" by Alfred Lord Tennyson.

PROLOGUE

When the Japanese Imperial Navy struck at Pearl Harbor American men responded by joining the military services. Many selected the Reserve components of the United States Navy and the Coast Guard, which was under control of the Navy.[1] Then, and for a while longer, the Navy accepted only volunteers, but later it also took draftees. The Navy assigned some of these young men to training stations and duties that eventually led to their becoming crew members of then newly constructed submarine chasers, patrol craft, mine sweepers, gun boats, Cutters, and other small combat ships.

As the war progressed, more young men joined this force of small ship sailors to man the fleet of more than one thousand small war craft. Their primarily reservist crew members later dubbed this collection of vessels the Donald Duck Navy.

These small ships guarded the coastlines of the Americas against U-Boats, mines, and Nazi spies and agents sent ashore from submarines. They steamed across the Atlantic and Pacific Oceans escorting merchant convoys and stalking submarines. In Europe and among the Pacific Islands they did similar duties but also performed mine sweeping operations, picket duty, air-sea rescue activities, and many other functions. Then they swept mines at invasion beaches ahead of the other ships and landing craft. Some of them became beach control vessels leading landing craft to invasion beaches. After invasions they acted as picket ships to warn the fleet of and protect it from air attacks. The ships and their crews performed efficiently, stoically, and bravely and were a tribute to themselves, the United States Navy and Coast Guard, and their country.

The young men who served on small ocean going ships of the Navy and the Coast Guard of the United States during World War II were a special type. They were mostly reservists with no or little sea duty when they went aboard their ships. Despite their lack of experience they learned fast and performed all the missions the Navy assigned to them, many of which the designers of the ships and naval planners never dreamed of during their conception and construction.

The small craft which these men sailed included submarine chasers, escort ships, patrol vessels, gunboats, mine sweepers, and Cutters. During World War II most of those ships never had names, only numbers. Some of them received names after the war.

Compared to the larger battleships, carriers, cruisers, and even destroyers, destroyer escorts, corvettes, and frigates they were bantam craft. Because of their small size, life aboard them for their crews was crowded and cramped and allowed no privacy. Their sailors had little room for personal possessions they had accumulated since their first day in the service.

When an enlisted man arrived at his first station, Boot Camp,[2] and received his gear and uniforms, some Navy clerk thrust at him also a canvas hammock, a thin mattress, two mattress cases, a pillow, two pillow cases, and two cream colored woolen blankets. Appendix A contains a description and photographs of all the items an enlisted man received when he was indoctrinated into the Navy. These sparse items he lugged wherever he went, taking his bed with him, even aboard ship. For something in which to store his uniforms, work clothes, and personal items the clerk tossed him a gray, cylindrical, thirty-four inch high, thirteen inch diameter, canvas sack. It had a row of six stitched grommets around the opening at the top through which the sailor inserted a length of rope. With that he drew the neck of the bag closed and secured it with a square knot. This sack was his Sea Bag.

This Sea Bag was an enlisted man's primary possession because he kept in it all he owned, needed, or prized. His Sea Bag was his retainer for all he owned while in the service. Rummaging through its contents he could trace his career, ships and stations on which he had served, places he had visited, actions in which he had been engaged, friends he had made, and shipmates he had lost. In that sense then, the storehouse of his memories of his time in the naval service was his Sea Bag.[3]

At sea the little ships pitched, yawed, and rolled viciously like no other ships. Their decks were awash with water. Forecastles, pilot houses, and flying bridges took green water even in moderate seas let alone in storms. Despite their rough riding the ships weathered the worst of nature and the enemy, and their crews endured and fought the war as bravely as did sailors on bigger ships.

Though the complements of each of these small ships numbered from about twenty to two-hundred men,[4] there were so many of these small ships that small craft sailors were equivalent in numbers to capital ship sailors. But they did not get the recognition given to the crews of the larger ships. These small craft sailors were competent seamen and heroic fighters, but like all sailors, among them were musicians, poets, writers, artists, and craftsmen.

Creativity among sailors has a long history. Down through the ages men who have gone to sea have left their traces in yarns told, song and chanties sung, and art and handcrafts.

Travelers and warriors on land could leave their mark by changing the landscape, constructing monuments, and altering indigenous peoples through marriage or less civilized methods. The sea, however, is eternal in form. It is not malleable nor can one build easily on it, and it is not peopled. Sailors could not leave their mark on the sea. They left their mark, instead, in other ways such as by composing songs and poems, relating tales, drawing sketches, painting pictures, decorating their ships, and making handcrafted items and ship models.

During their days aboard the small ships in World War II, the men lived, worked, fought the enemy, stood watches, ate, and slept in close uncomfortable quarters with little time or space for private thoughts or actions. Yet, they, like former sailors, played music and wrote, drew, painted, and crafted items that were original, humorous, and artistic. It is a tribute to these men that, despite the limitations on their personal lives, their restricted freedom of thought and action, and the dangers that confronted them, they found the time and the mental and physical discipline to compose and construct what they did. Their original works are not only tributes to them but to the tenacity of the human creative spirit.

The strains of their music, songs, and tales are no longer with us, but some of their material work still exists.

Some small amount of it is available for public view, scattered throughout museums. Much of it is in personal collections and not known to the public and historians. These items should be displayed to the public and preserved as part of the history of the young men who served on the small ocean-going ships of the Navy and Coast Guard of the United States in World War II.

This book is my contribution to the preservation and recorded history of some of those original creations generated by the small ship sailors of World War II. With this collection I hope I have helped the current generation and will help future generations learn what those young men created under such adverse conditions. I also hope I have opened, explored among, and made available, for those erstwhile young men, treasures from their Sea Bag of Memories.

THE SEA BAG

There was a time when everything you owned had to fit in your Sea Bag. Remember those nasty rascals? Fully packed, one of the sonsabitches weighed more than the poor devil hauling it. The Army, Marines and Air Force got footlockers and we in the Navy and Coast Guard got a big old canvas bag.

After you warped your spine jackassing the goofy thing through a bus or train station, sat on it waiting for connecting transportation, and made folks mad because it was too big to fit in an overhead rack on any bus or train, the contents looked like hell. All your gear appeared to have come from bums who slept on park benches.

Traveling with a seabag was something left over from the, "yo-ho-ho and a bottle of rum," sailing ship days. Sailors used to sleep in hammocks. So you stowed your issue in a big canvas bag and lashed your hammock to it, hoisted it on your shoulder and moved all your possessions from ship to ship.

I wouldn't say you traveled light because it was a one-shoulder load that could torque your skeletal form and bust your ankles. It was like hauling a dead linebacker.

They wasted a lot of time in boot camp telling you how to pack one of the sonsabitches. There was an officially sanctioned method of organization that you forgot after ten minutes on the other side of the gate at Great Lakes. You got rid of a lot of issue gear when you went aboard ship.

Did you ever know a sailor who had a raincoat? A flat hat? One of those knit swimsuits? Within six months every sailor was down to one set of dress blues, port and starboard undress blues and whites, a couple of rag hats, boots, shoes, assorted skivvies, a pea coat, and three sets of leper colony-looking dungarees. The rest of your original issue was either in the lucky bag or had been reduced to wipe down rags in the engine room.

Do they still issue sea bags? Can you still draw an anchor on the side of one of the damn things with a black pen that would drive an old master-at-arms into a, "rig for heart attack," frenzy and yell, "What in God's name is that all over your Sea Bag?"

"Artwork, Chief it's like the work of Michelangelo. Great huh?"

"Looks like some gahdam comic book."

Sometimes I look at all the crap stacked in my garage, close my eyes, and smile remembering a time when everything I owned could be crammed into a canvas bag.

This essay was excerpted and modified from one that has appeared in other variations. The version adapted here was courtesy of Jack Hogan.

INTRODUCTION

Many types of small vessels served in the Navy and Coast Guard of the United States during World War II. Some were harbor craft such as barges, tug boats, and net tenders. Others were coastal vessels the Navy used for patrol and miscellaneous tasks outside of the harbors but close to shore. These types included converted yachts and other small craft. Also there were many other small ocean going ships including landing craft.

All these ships had crew members who served just as faithfully and gallantly as those on larger craft, and they too had their poets and artists. Their efforts and works should be recognized. In this book, however, because of the need to limit the size and scope of the book, I consider only the works of the small ocean going ships listed on the next page. These ships sailed and fought while escorting convoys, doing antisubmarine patrols, sweeping for mines, controlling landing craft to invasion beaches, and performing many other tasks in every ocean and in all theaters of the war.

Those Navy ships classified as ocean going small craft that I consider in this book are:

Submarine Chasers: Patrol Craft (PC), Patrol Craft Control (PCC), Patrol Craft Escort (PCE), Patrol Craft Escort Communications (PCEC), Patrol Craft Escort Rescue (PCER), Submarine Chaser (SC), and Submarine Chaser Control (SCC).

Patrol Vessels: Yard Patrol (YP), Yacht (PY), and Coastal Yacht (PYc),

Minesweepers: Fleet Minesweeper (AM), Patrol Craft Sweeper (PCS), Fleet mine sweepers (AM, ex PC and ex SC), and Auxiliary Motor Minesweeper (YMS).

Gunboats: Motor Gunboats (PGM, ex PC and ex SC).

Cutters: In addition to the Navy ships listed above, some of which were manned by Coast Guard crews, the Coast Guard operated and manned Cutters that were built before World War II and reclassified. Those considered in this book include Submarine Chaser (WPC), and Submarine Chaser (WSC). Further information about Coast Guard ships is in other books including the books about the Coast Guard listed in the Bibliography.

At least one photograph of each type of these ships is given in Appendix B. Specifications for these ships are given in Appendix C. Other sources of material about these small ships are given in the Bibliography. Additional information about them can be found on the internet using the URLs listed in the section titled Related Websites.

After World War II many of the former small ship sailors continued to generate original work that depicted or reflected on their years aboard ship. Some of these items also are included in this record. I also have included in this book material from sources other than small ship sailors. These items were made by persons associated with the construction of the ships and training of the crews, or they augment and illustrate the recognition and appreciation of these special small ship sailors by the originators of the material. I include those works by other persons, regardless of when the persons did them, in Chapter X titled Other Contributors. Because the works referred to in this paragraph were done by former small ship sailors after World War II, I include them in Chapter XII titled The Later Years.

NOTE TO THE READER

I regret that many of the figures in this book are not of high quality. There are numerous reasons. Photographs were from old, black and white, withered, faded copies with imperfections. Drawings were old and faded, sometimes folded and wrinkled, and often they were fifty-year old mimeographed copies of originals. Paintings were second or third copies of originals.

In all cases digital scanning and improvements helped to improve their quality.

CHAPTER I

THE DONALD DUCK NAVY

Sailors who served during World War II on small ocean going ships of the United States Navy and Coast Guard that became known as the Donald Duck Navy had mixed feelings at first about the epithet "Donald Duck." This was because most, if not all, of the men were familiar with the Walt Disney cartoon creation named Donald Duck. Because of their memories of Donald Duck as a comic character, at first they thought the name was uncomplimentary and even degrading. Also, other sailors who served on larger ships, who did not understand the difficulties of being a small ship sailor, often used the term "Donald Duck Navy" in a derogatory manner.

Eventually, though, most men who served on the small ships developed pride in their ships and cherished the camaraderie of their crews, and they gloried in the duck symbol[5] because it identified them as an unique group of rugged sailors.

The origin of the use of the name "Donald Duck Navy" is obscure and is debated even today by former sailors and historians. Some reliable evidence and anecdotal accounts indicate that its use started at the Submarine Chaser Training Center (SCTC) in Miami, Florida.[6] Though the United States Navy established and operated other training centers for men who would man small craft and mine sweepers in Norfolk, Virginia and elsewhere, SCTC was the focal point and the most important one for training crews for the subchaser fleet. By the end of the war, more than 50,000 enlisted men and officers of the United States Navy, Coast Guard, and Allied Navies had endured rigorous training at SCTC.

The symbol of a duck appeared on letterheads, notices, signs, bulletin boards, ships' superstructures, and, without official acceptance, on some sailors' uniforms.

SUBMARINE CHASER TRAINING CENTER
MIAMI, FLORIDA

Figure I-1. This figure shows a Letterhead used for correspondence from the Submarine Chaser Training Center (SCTC) in Miami, Florida. The photograph is courtesy of James McMahon.

Figure I-2. This is a bulletin board poster at the Submarine Chaser Training Center in Miami, Florida. The photograph is from the author's collection.

Figure I-3. Jim Dickie, Signalman on PC 564 (USS *Chadron*), made this fighting duck insignia. It also appeared, without the PC 564 numbers and with ground under its feet, on the letterhead used at SCTC. The drawing is courtesy of William (Bill) Buffington.

Figure I-4. This insignia was used on PC1242. The drawing is by and courtesy of Bill Buffington.

Figure I-5. This insignia of a duck in the crow's nest was used on PC 546. It was drawn in ink and painted on the starboard side at the entrance to the bridge. It is courtesy of George Amaral.

Figure I-6. This photograph shows a patch some sailors wore on their uniforms. The Navy did not authorize the patch, and sailors discontinued using it because the wearer would be out of uniform and subject to discipline. It is shown in color in the Section titled Color Plates. The photograph is courtesy of Jim McMahon.

These six symbols are only a few of the many duck type insignia that other ships, stations, and sailors used in various ways. They are, however, a representative cross section of the interest in and use of the duck figure by small ship sailors to show their pride in their ships and themselves and of being part of what they proudly called the Donald Duck Navy.

CHAPTER II

OTHER SHIP INSIGNIA

Though many small ship sailors decorated their ships with variations of the duck image as shown in Chapter I, some of them preferred insignia different from the duck in various poses. Sailors of some small ships drew, used in posters, and painted on their ships cartoons involving other animals. Some even used insects in the figures. Three of these designs are shown on the next two pages.

During World War II aircraft crews of the United States Army Air Corps graced many of their bombers' noses with pinup girl figures. Some were like commercial figures such as those generated by George Petty and Alberto Vargas. Others were original paintings done by the servicemen. Their work, decorating the noses of bombers, had been well publicized in writing and by photographs in military and civilian newspapers and in Newsreels shown in stateside theaters, and these figures continued to be noted after the war. Not to be outdone by the Army flyers some patrol craft and other small ship sailors also enhanced their ships' superstructures with colorful images of beautiful women. One such image is shown in Figure II-4.

Figure II-1. This rendition of Porky Pig appeared on PC 1225. The drawing was by and is courtesy of Bill Buffington.

Figure II-2. This image of a Bull Dog ready to ram a shell into a gun was used on PC 565. The drawing was by and is courtesy of Bill Buffington.

Figure II-3. This insignia of a bee prepared to drop depth charges was designed by Alfred (Don) Macdonald, QM 3/C for use on SC 734 in 1943. The photograph is courtesy of Mrs. Elsie Macdonald.

Figure II-4. An insignia depicting a scantily clad young lady was painted on the superstructure of PC 616. Sid Frey painted the figure. The photograph is courtesy of Rick Reynolds.

Subchaser sailors also enjoyed showing their disdain for the enemy and how they would attack and defeat enemy submarines. One sketch shows a drawing of a picture that was to be painted on the superstructure of a PC.

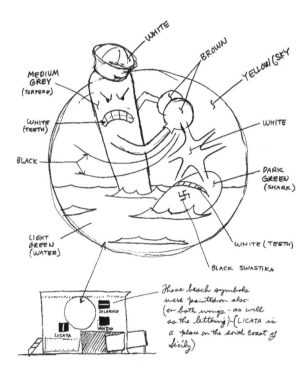

Figure II-5. This sketch depicts an American ship as a sailor and torpedo knocking out a Nazi U-boat shark. It was drawn in the Mediterranean and is courtesy of the Patrol Craft Sailors Association.

During World War II various agencies of the United States government created posters and cartoons to stimulate defiance of and hatred for the leaders of the Axis governments. Hitler, Mussolini, and Tojo became favorite characters in these posters. In addition to using animals and other images on ships, some sailors used them in other ways to ridicule the rulers of the Axis governments. One such cartoon is shown here.

Figure II-6. Seen here is Bugs Bunny taking vengeance on General Tojo who became the Premier of the Imperial Japanese government. It was drawn by Norm Helford and is courtesy of Donald F. Townsend. Both men served on PC 590.

These insignia and cartoons gave the men on the small ships of the United States Navy and Coast Guard an identity that made them feel different from the many other similar ships. They did not want to be just one small item in a large group. They wanted individual recognition. The images they painted on their ships made them feel that their ships were special and that they were individuals.

CHAPTER III

TRAINING SMALL SHIP SAILORS

As the involvement of the United States in World War II progressed, the United States Navy built thousands of small ships. The Navy had to rapidly turn hundreds of thousands of recruits into sailors to man these ships as the ships poured out of shipyards and onto the oceans. To accomplish this goal the Navy quickly built and staffed more recruit training stations, called Boot Camps, for enlisted men and officer indoctrination schools around the country to supplement the ones already in existence.

For enlisted recruits their first taste of navy life was Boot Camp. Here they doffed their civvies and struggled to learn how to slither into a tight blue jumper, squeeze into trousers with bells on the bottom and thirteen buttons, and how to lace leggings with the hooks on the outside. They had their long hair clipped almost to the bone. They winced as needles jabbed their arms with all kinds of inoculations. They learned to say, "Sir," to any one with a uniform different from theirs. They marched, scrubbed clothing, tied knots, slung rifles, studied points of the compass, scrubbed decks, smoked only when the "Smoking Lamp" was lit, and fought off sleep as they stood mid-watches with shouldered rifles inside and outside of their barracks.

Then they had their first encounter with a Navy Disbursing Officer, the officer who would issue their pay. Through him they met the infamous "Flying Five." After shuffling slowly along a long line of other recruits each man signed his name to a pay ledger. The officer handed him a crisp new five dollar bill as a down payment on his first month's pay of twenty-one dollars. When shuffled off to the next station, a Petty Officer snatched the five dollar bill from the Boot and thrust a canvas ditty bag at him. In it were soap, toothpaste, a tooth brush, and shaving gear. He was ushered to the next Petty Officer who handed him a few cents change from the "Flying Five" and rushed him off to join his other bewildered and moneyless buddies.

Most of the new Navy and Coast Guard men who entered these Boot Camps, training stations, and officer candidate schools had never been to sea, and many had never even seen an ocean or a ship. In a short time, though, they had to learn all that was necessary to sail and fight a ship of war. On entry to the Navy, however, they knew very little about oceans, ships, guns, and the ways of the Navy.[7]

After they finished Boot Camp, some of these men the Navy sent directly to shore stations or even aboard ships. Most enlisted men, however, went to other training centers for advanced seamanship, gunnery, and general naval practices. Many also went to Navy or factory schools to be trained in specialties in which they would receive Petty Officer rates.

The Petty Office rates for sailors who served on small ships, in alphabetical order, with some typical nicknames for them, included:

Boatswain's Mate (Boats, Deck Ape)
Coxswain (Deck Ape)
Electrician's Mate (Bulb Snatcher, Sparks)
Fireman (Snipe, Bilge Rat)
Gunner's Mate (Guns)
Mess Cook
Motor Machinist's Mate (Snipe, member of the Black
    Gang)
Pharmacist's Mate (Pills, Pecker Checker)
Quartermaster (Wheels)
Radarman (Scope Jockey)
Radioman (Sparks)
Seaman (Deck Ape, Swabby)
Shipfitter
Ship's Cook (Cookie)
Signalman (Flags, Skivvy Waver)
Sonarman (Ping Jockey)
Officer's Steward
Storekeeper (Keys)
Yeoman (Pens).

Many men who had college educations received commissions from various sources as officers in the Navy and Coast Guard. Generally they were commissioned as Ensign. Some officer candidates with specialties such as engineering, medicine, law, and intelligence received ranks higher than Ensign. Regardless of rank, however, they all received some naval indoctrination, basic training, and advanced training.

Aboard the small United States navy ships of World War II typical billets assigned to commissioned officers were as listed here. Some of their less formal names also are shown.

Commanding Officer (Captain, Skipper, Old Man)
Medical Officer (Usually the Captain)
Chaplain (Padre, Usually the Captain)
Executive Officer (XO)
First Lieutenant (Often the XO)
Navigation Officer
Gunnery Officer
Engineering Officer
Communications Officer

Often the most junior officer aboard ship also performed collateral duties such as morale, laundry, and commissary officer.

Navy training schools, such as the "A" and "C" basic and advanced schools, for enlisted men were established in many places around the United States. They were highly efficient, and their staffs trained new sailors rapidly in the rates given above. Some men also went to factory schools such as those run by General Motors to train men on their Diesel engines.

All the schools used lectures, reading material, shop sessions, field and shipboard exercises, and hands-on training. Trainees at the schools received written material and manuals they studied and on which the staffs tested them periodically.

Also, instructors usually required the trainees to keep their own personal notebooks containing material on which they were being instructed. The school instructors examined these notebooks periodically. Men who completed training at schools were graded by their work in class and on the notebooks, and their standing relative to the other trainees in their class was graded and entered into their service jackets. These service jacket entries contributed to the selection of men for promotion to higher rates.

The instruction manuals given to the trainees were professionally written, detailed, and complete, and they presented the material clearly. For example, the next figure shows a page from a Diesel School training manual depicting the Control Diagram for a Fairbanks Morse Diesel engine.

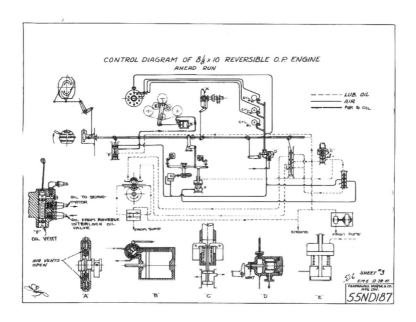

Figure III-1. This is a diagram of the "ahead run" position of controls for a Fairbanks Morse main propulsion Diesel Engine on a PC. It is from a manual at a Navy Diesel School attended by Elra J. Reitz and is courtesy of Michael Reitz.

From their attendance at these schools, the sailors in training became rated Petty Officers, generally Third Class[8] but sometimes Second Class. Usually schools lasted from one to a few months. At the end of their instruction the trainees became knowledgeable in their jobs and qualified to handle their tasks for their rate aboard ship. However, not all of the trainees, overcame certain tendencies to be a bit lax in the application of their training to their ratings and jobs aboard ship.

Figure III-2. This cartoon shows the tendency of sailors who had trained as Signalmen to use "informal" language in their duties. The officer is reading the words, "Page 22 of the BLUEJACKETS' MANUAL, 1940, 10th Edition states: PROFANITY–Men are profane usually because they lack education and need profane words to express themselves forcibly or because they are naturally evil-minded. In either case men using profane or filthy language have something lacking for development . . . etc." The drawing is by and is courtesy of Bill Buffington.

Most small ships used Diesel engines for propulsion and for generating electric power. Some ships used gasoline engines.

For both types of engines the Navy sent men to schools to train as Motor Machinist Mates (MoMM). The training was successful. Many young men who had no previous knowledge of internal combustion engines or other machinery learned what they had to know at these schools. After they went aboard ship they operated, maintained, and repaired their ship's engines and other machinery. Their efforts and knowledge enabled their crews to take small ships across oceans and back safely. Of course not all the men learned all they needed to know to care for their engines as depicted in the following cartoon.

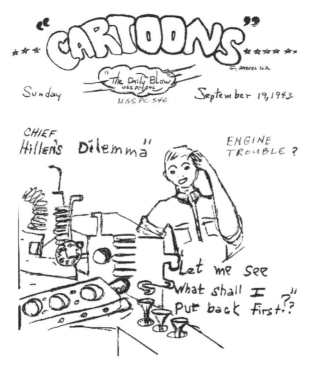

Figure III-3. Here the Chief Motor Machinist Mate ponders how to reassemble an engine. This cartoon was in The Daily Blow a ship's newspaper published on PC 546 on Sunday, September 19, 1943. It is courtesy of George Amaral.

The Navy drew its influx of commissioned officers from the Naval Academy and college, university Reserve Officer Training Corps (ROTC) programs, and from the enlisted ranks. The supply was inadequate however, so the Navy established various officer training programs for men with college degrees or some college education. The Navy sent selectees in these programs through a ninety day indoctrination program from which the graduates received commissions, most as Ensigns. They became known in the Navy as the "Ninety Day Wonders." Despite minimal training most of them went on to serve effectively.

Both officers and enlisted men assigned to the ships of the Donald Duck Navy got further training in mine warfare and antisubmarine warfare. On the west coast one school familiar to many patrol craft sailors was the West Coast Sound School at Point Loma, San Diego, California. There, officers and men got practice finding and "attacking" real United States Navy submarines. Three East Coast areas used for small ship training were the Mine Warfare Training Center and the Small Craft Training Center in Norfolk, Virginia and the Submarine Chaser Training Center (SCTC) in Miami, Florida.

SCTC was the primary site for training men to fight submarines. At SCTC, enlisted men received instruction and hands-on training in seamanship, gunnery, and other skills to become a fighting crew on a subchaser. Though most of the trainees excelled in their new skills, they were the targets of friendly joshing by instructors at SCTC. Some of this joking was displayed in cartoons in the training manual that the instructors used at SCTC.[9]

HOWS TO WAIT FOR OUR "READY LIGHTS" NEXT TIME

Figure III-4. Being expert at using a subchaser's weapons was essential to fighting submarines. This cartoon is from the <u>Submarine Chaser Manual 1942 Second Edition</u>. It is courtesy of Linda Wheeler of the Hoover Institution Library at Stanford University.

"LOOK SKIPPER - NO HANDS"

Figure III-5. Competent helmsmen were essential to a skipper intent on stalking a submarine. This cartoon is from the <u>Submarine Chaser Manual 1942 Second Edition</u>. It is courtesy of Linda Wheeler of the Hoover Institution Library at Stanford University.

All I hear is three toots on a siren and the words "Modern Design"

Figure III-6. With experts on the sound gear a submarine could not escape a subchaser. This cartoon is from the <u>Submarine Chaser Manual 1942 Second Edition</u>. It is courtesy of Linda Wheeler of the Hoover Institution Library at Stanford University.

"Literally Decoded, Gentlemen, It says, 'Nuts To Us'."

Figure III-7. Signalmen were given instructions to be explicit and detailed about messages relayed to officers. This cartoon is from the <u>Submarine Chaser Manual 1942 Second Edition</u>. It is courtesy of Linda Wheeler of the Hoover Institution Library at Stanford University.

Officers got training similar to but more advanced in some matters than that of the enlisted men. The "Bible" for officer training at SCTC was the Submarine Chaser Manual. Cartoons in the manual also took swipes at the capability of the officers in training as shown in figures on the next four pages.

"Alright, Swami, What's Our Next Guess?"

Figure III-8. Ship handling was essential to a young officer. He always requested and got the best advice from senior officers as shown here. This cartoon is from the <u>Submarine Chaser Manual 1942 Second Edition</u>. It is courtesy of Linda Wheeler of the Hoover Institution Library at Stanford University.

You Know Captain, I'm Beginning to Doubt My Noon Position, Too

Figure III-9. Crossing an ocean was no problem with a good navigator aboard. This cartoon is from the <u>Submarine Chaser Manual 1942 Second Edition.</u> It is courtesy of Linda Wheeler of the Hoover Institution Library at Stanford University.

Just Give Me One Reason Why We Can't Get Underway

Figure III-10. A competent engineering officer understood his machinery and the men in his black gang. This cartoon is from the Submarine Chaser Manual 1942 Second Edition. It is courtesy of Linda Wheeler of the Hoover Institution Library at Stanford University.

"Mulvaney, You're A Bottleneck in Our Expansion Program"

Figure III-11. This drawing shows how not to get the best effort from one of the black gang. This cartoon is from the <u>Submarine Chaser Manual 1942 Second Edition.</u> It is courtesy of Linda Wheeler of the Hoover Institution Library at Stanford University.

Despite all the cartoons, jokes, and friendly ridicule men and officers received from their instructors and other sailors, they learned their lessons well. The vast majority of them, enlisted men and commissioned officers, went on to their shipboard and other assignments and performed their duties as needed. They sailed their small ships with competence, fought the oceans' torments, survived the worst of storms, and braved the enemy. They succeeded as well as did other Navy and Coast Guard men on larger ships, and some of them gained rapid promotions, assumed important positions, and accepted great responsibilities. For what the trainees and the men who trained them did they deserve a Well Done.

CHAPTER IV

LIFE ABOARD A SMALL SHIP

Hefting his Sea Bag and mattress over his shoulder and striding across the gangplank and onto the deck of a sailor's first ship gave a young man a thrill he would never forget.[10] This experience was especially true if he were a Plank Owner – one of the members of the original crew that was aboard when the Navy commissioned the ship.

Plank Owner or not, the first tasks a new "hand" performed were to locate his bunk and locker, make up his sack, and stow his gear. After that he located the other two most important compartments on the ship – the head and the mess hall. Then he could take the time to find his work station and learn the intricacies of where he would stand his watches. Next came his time to read the Watch, Quarter, and Station Bill to find his duties and locations on the ship for various evolutions such as General Quarters (battle stations), man overboard, and other crisis type situations. As time allowed, he would then explore and learn about all the other parts of his new home.

Members of the black gang – the engineers – did not have this luxury of time. For the ship to operate and survive they had to learn immediately and remember where every water, oil, fuel, and flushing line went and where the control valves were located. They did this by crawling through compartments and bilges and making sketches of all pipe lines and other related machinery. This knowledge they committed to memory. A typical sketch made by one of them is shown.

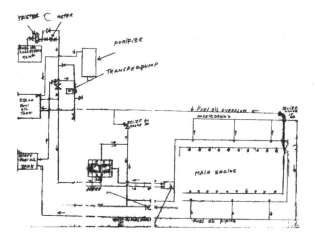

Figure IV-1. This sketch of the fuel oil piping system on PC 466 was drawn by Elra John Reitz and is courtesy of Michael Reitz.

Other duties the seamen or "Deck Apes" took part in were fitting the ship and preparing lines and fenders. They took great pride in "whipping" the lifelines, ladder railings, and other parts so men could get a safer grip on them. Also, they wove "monkey fists" (one is shown in Baldwin's Plate 15 in the Section Titled Plates) on the end of heaving lines,[11] and they wove their own fenders that hung over the side when the ship was moored against a dock or another ship. The following two pictures show a man weaving a fender and the pride he took in making it.

Figure IV-2. This photograph shows an unidentified sailor weaving a fender.

Figure IV-3. In this photograph the sailor is seen showing his pride in and affection for the fender he wove.

After men and officers knew their stations and learned their duties, the drills for emergency conditions such as fire aboard ship, man overboard, collision, and battle stations (General Quarters or GQ) became an important part of their training. Also of prime importance was for the officers to learn to con the ship especially coming alongside a dock to tie up. They quickly became proficient at this maneuver, especially if they had a seamanlike crew to help as shown in the figure on this page.

Figure IV-4. This cartoon shows a not too salty crew undergoing a "Chinese Fire Drill" while trying to dock the ship. It was drawn by a cartoonist named Card, and is courtesy of Jack Hogan.

Duty aboard a small ship was especially difficult for sailors because of the lack of space for themselves and their possessions and invasion of their privacy that stretched their patience. Violent motions of the ship, even when tied up to a dock, agitated the mens' stomachs and equilibrium making seasickness an almost constant condition for many men. The cartoon on the next page illustrates the problem men had getting their "sea legs."

MAL DE MER (FR.)   FIRST DAY OUT ON A SUBCHASER

Figure IV-5. This scene was common on small ships. It was drawn by Darrell McClure and is courtesy of Bob Daly and Theodore Treadwell.

Constant exposure to spindrift from heavy seas and strong wind and changeable and often foul weather brought on cases of respiratory problems. Navy medics, Corpsmen, and even medical doctors usually called it CAT[12] fever and invariably treated it with APC pills. And there were other health problems from injuries and enemy actions.

Then too, there was the dull routine of standing watches, four hours on and eight hours off, that at times seemed endless, especially when the ship was on Ping Patrol guarding harbors against enemy submarines or escorting convoys across the oceans. Or men manned their battle stations for hours waiting for action to start or being in the thick of it, standing in either hot or cold weather with little nourishing food or drink and no chance to rest.

In port and even at sea, besides standing watch, the crew always had plenty of work to do to maintain and repair damage to their ship. They longed to do other personal things but rarely had the time. Ship's work always came first. Most of all, though, they wanted to let the folks back home know where they were what they were doing, and about their lives. But, the censors, who were the officers aboard the ships, prevented them from doing that. Censorship was necessary to keep the enemy from inadvertently getting information on ship and troop movements and dispositions.

Some of the characteristics, problems, and longings of the men, and the issue of censorship imposed on them, are expressed in the following poem.

AIN'T IT THE TRUTH

I sit down to write with so much to say,
But how can I tell it when there isn't a way:
Can't say where I'm at, censors, you know,
Can't say where we've been – or where we may go.
Can't talk 'bout the sights, or what we have met,
Can't talk 'bout the ship or the food that we get;
Can't smoke after dark, must go early to bed,
Can't use any flashlights – must rely on your head.
Can't write love and XXX might be in code,
Can't talk about battle or seas we've out-rode;
Can't tell of the sunshine, the rain or the storm,
Can't say if we're freezing or whether we're warm.
Can't do many things, but this we can do –
We can eat, we can sleep – when they tell us to;
We can laugh and be merry, but can't overdo it,
We can tell folks we're happy,

and hope they'll not see through it.
We could p l a y the radio – but we haven't got one,
We could get a good tan, if we just had the sun;
We could sit aft and fish, but there's never a bite,
We could argue for hours, but it ends in a fight.
We can go ashore, but there's nothing there,
We can grow a beard, but we can't have long hair;
We can tell jokes for hours – but I don't know any,
We can borrow from friends,
but those "With" aren't many.
We can do all these things and perhaps many others,
But we want only one thing – and that, my dear brothers,
Is to finish this fight and return home again,
To where women are women, and men were once men.
And in later years we may laugh at all this,
And there may be a time when we'll find that we'll miss
Some of this life, that w e know so well,
And may wish we were back a board – who can tell.

This poem was written by Tony Rego.

Aboard a small United States ship the Navy expected the commissioned officers to use wisdom and censor their own written messages to persons at home. They also shared the duty of censoring the enlisted men's mail, hacking out words with scissors or obliterating them with black ink. It was difficult for them to have to read and learn about the personal issues of members of the crew, but it was more trying for the enlisted men whose personal thoughts were exposed to a third party, who had military jurisdiction over them.

Men either refrained from writing about very personal issues, or they tried to hide their messages in prearranged codes with friends, family, wives, or girl friends. These attempts at coded messages generally were unwieldy and not too successful. This failure to get messages delivered left the sailors and the recipients of their mail frustrated.

Writing to loved ones was especially difficult on anniversaries of family events, birthdays, holidays, or on special occasions. Valentine's Day was one of those special occasions when service men overseas thought of their girls at home and tried to send messages of their love to their girl friends. One man's original Valentine Day greeting that he sent to his favorite lady at home got the censor's black ink treatment as shown in the figure on this page.

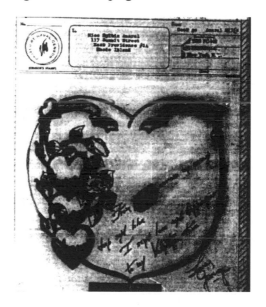

Figure IV-6. This V-Mail card reads, "From (censored) across an ocean deep and blue, I send love and happiness to my Valentine true." This greeting was sent by George Amaral, SK 2/C, from PC 546 in the Mediterranean in 1943. It is courtesy of George Amaral

Another original V-mail celebrating the Holiday Season that no one censored is shown here. Note that it was mailed through the Fleet Post Office, New York, New York. That address was a "clearing house" for overseas mail in the Atlantic and Mediterranean. All ships and stations in this theater of war used this address. Ships in the Pacific theater of war used a similar address in San Francisco. The government used these addresses so the location of the sources of the mail sent to the States could not be identified by the enemy. In effect this also was a form of censorship, but it was not an objectionable one to servicemen and their families and friends at home.

Figure IV-7. This V Mail Christmas Greeting to his mother and father was drawn by George Amaral on December 11, 1943 on PC 546 in the Mediterranean. It is courtesy of George Amaral.

Large ships had facilities aboard to ease the lives of their crews and to take care of menial tasks. Most of them had a ship's store that sold cigarettes, candy, stationary, and personal items. They had a number of other services such as a barber shop, a laundry, and a tailor. The smaller vessels did not have room aboard for such amenities. A ship's store was most likely a locker in the mess hall that an assigned crew member opened for an hour or so on selected days. For hair cuts men perched in the open on ammunition lockers or any convenient object while their buddies butchered their hair with dull scissors.

Figure IV-8. This sketch shows a typical "barber shop" on a small ship. It was drawn by a cartoonist named Card and is courtesy of Jack Hogan.

At times men "washed" their dungarees by tying them to a heaving line and trailing them behind the ship. This method was fine at slow speeds, but resulted in shredded rags if the ship speeded up. Most sailors used a more traditional method and scrubbed their clothes in a metal bucket with salt water. To get a lather, instead of using conventional sodium-based soap, they sliced chips from a cake of potassium-based soap called "salt water soap" or "sailors' soap."

On some ships the crews contributed money and bought washing machines they installed in the head. Because of limited space, however, the washing machine was no larger than a small family size washer, though it served up to about sixty men. Officers had stewards who did their laundry for them in many cases. When they could, officers had the stewards leave laundry at shore stations to be done for them.

Dryers did not exist. Crew members hung wet clothing to dry wherever they could find space. Topside was preferred if the weather permitted and the skipper did not object. If not topside then the men found other places. It was not unusual to see damp skivvies hanging from the springs under a man's bunk or, though it was frowned on, at a watch station. Engineers profited in this regard by the heat in the engine room and the draft created by engine air intakes. Frequently the snipes decorated the engine rooms with freshly washed clothing hanging from pipe lines and draped over the work bench.

Small ship sailors did not have tailors available so enlisted men and often even the commissioned officers had to find a convenient space to sit and make their own repairs to their uniforms, or sew on chevrons after getting a promotion, as shown in the figure on the next page.

NOV. 19 1943
PC 1228

Douglas P. Spade

Figure IV-9. This figure is of a man sewing his uniform. It shows a typical enlisted man's living compartment with double or triple decker cots and small lockers each man used to store his uniforms and all else he owned. The drawing was made on 19 November 1943 on PC 1228 by Douglas P. Spade.

Despite the cramped and uncomfortable life aboard a small ship the men enjoyed one privilege rarely found on a large Navy ship. Duty on a small ship was less formal than that on carriers, battleships, and other large ships. Officers rarely required or received salutes, enlisted men and commissioned officers fraternized and developed friendships, and uniform requirements were relaxed. Particularly, on capital ships, the quarterdeck at the gangway was sacred ground, and sailors on duty there wore dress uniforms. The following figure shows an enlisted man standing a quarterdeck watch on a small ship in a somewhat informal uniform.

Figure IV-10. This sketch was done by Kenneth A. Hooks on PC 1228 when he returned from liberty and made a pencil drawing of his shipmate, Ed Comeau, on gangway watch. Later he rendered it in ink. It shows the hooded box used to protect the log from weather, the base of a canvas covered 20mm antiaircraft machine gun, and the ship's boat.

Not only on the quarterdeck but almost anywhere and at any time the men on small ships wore less than regulation uniforms.

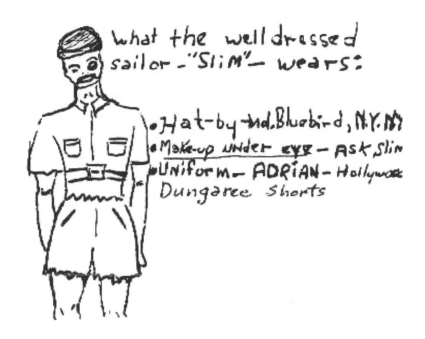

Figure IV-11. This cartoon of what the well dressed sailor "Slim" wears was in The Daily Blow a ship's paper on PC 546, Sunday, September 19, 1943. It is courtesy of George Amaral.

One of the benefits of serving on a small ship was the relaxed atmosphere. Another one was that the food was usually hearty, healthful, and plentiful. Many ships had open galleys at night when anyone could fix a snack or even a short meal for himself. Cooks generally did their utmost to show their culinary ability and to keep the crew happy. Food was plentiful, except for certain commodities.

Fresh fruit, fresh vegetables, and fresh dairy products were in short supply. After weeks, months, and years of the gummy consistency and foul taste of powdered eggs, a real egg was a rare treat. The same was true of other products as shown in the next cartoon.

Fresh Butter!! and hands across the Table. Take it easy Boys??

Figure. IV-12. This cartoon showing a sailor's special interest in fresh butter was in <u>The Daily Blow</u> a ship's paper on PC 546, Sunday, September 19, 1943. It is courtesy of George Amaral.

Captains of all ships called upon sailors to perform many tasks, called evolutions. Sailors enjoyed some of them like "mail call" or "liberty party away." Other evolutions, such as "loading ammunition" or "taking on stores," they disliked because they entailed hard work or took the men away from their free time. But the evolution sailors disliked most was "inspection."

Duty, weather, and enemy action permitting, most skippers of small ships inspected their ships weekly or on some regular schedule. The enlisted men hated having this task take away their spare time or time needed for repairs and maintenance and instead require them to clean, dust, sweep, chip, paint, oil, and otherwise pretty a ship.

Worse than that, though, was personnel inspection. This meant digging dress uniforms from the bottom of Sea Bags and lockers, sleeping on them under one's mattress to crease them, spit shining black shoes worn only for liberty, and scrubbing white hats. The uniforms that the hands wore for inspection hardly resembled or seemed to be related to the daily uniform of foul weather gear, Marine boondocker shoes, watch caps, dungarees, shorts, skivvie shirts, or less that was typically worn aboard ship.

The men understood that the basic intention of inspection was to keep a vessel shipshape and for hygiene. Those goals seemed, to many men, to be less a reason and more of an excuse for personnel inspection. The real reason – they bitched about inspection – was that it was an excuse to let the skipper and other officers exert their authority and make life more miserable for the enlisted men. The following poem captures some of the essence of that opinion of a personnel inspection.

INSPECTION'S COMIN'

"Fall in youse guys'n make it fast, the captain's
comin' soon –
Inspection's set for nine o'clock, but twill
probably be at noon!"

"Hey there mac – square that hat,'n fix your
gawdamned tie! –
You'll get restricted right off the bat, if you catch
the "skipper's eye.""

"Seaman! – cripes look at them shoes, and the
cuff that's on them pants – I hate forever to sing
the blues – but no wonder the ol' man rants!"

"Pockets full of gigs an' gum,'n a chin that's full
of beard –
This ain't no place to be "for fun"– it's the Navy,
or ain't you heard!"

"Stand by now mates – toe that line, at ease stand
if you will –
By gawd you're lookin' mighty fine – gives this
ol' "Boats" a thrill!"

"When the' spection party hits the bridge, it's
attention and hand salute,
And the guy who messes up on this, gets a fine –
and duty to boot!"

"Front line three steps up 'y march, now square
off best you can,
Allowin room for that big gun arch an' standin'
away from that pan!"

"Now stand right still, don't move your feet – else
you'll never get back in line –
I wish to gawd those guys would come – this
seems a waste of time!"

"It's rainin' now but what the hell, you guys is
used to water –
So what? Your whites is gettin' wet – did you
want the captain's daughter?"

"Quiet now men – here's the Exec." - - - - My
gawd this life's a pain,
"Inspection's off" – He just now said, on
accounta' all this rain!!!

This poem was written in 1944 by Phil Donahue, Y2/C
USNR, who served on PC 623 in the Pacific area. It was quoted
in the PCSA News, Issue Number 9, Page 10.

Though cleansing the ship and keeping the men clean
was in the interests of hygiene, occasionally there was a crew
member who never seemed to want to wash. His shipmates
usually took care of the matter, however, without the need for
intervention by the officers. The following cartoon mentions one
method by which the crew maintained personal hygiene of
reluctant shipmates.

Figure IV-13. This cartoon suggesting a method for enforcing personal hygiene by hosing a man down or dragging him from the fantail was drawn by, and is courtesy of William Buffington.

Christmas day always had special significance for men aboard a United States naval ship, especially if they were at sea during Christmas day. The time was an occasion to remind the men of home and the pleasures of family life they no longer enjoyed. Many of the men tried to capture the spirit of what Christmas was like at home by attending religious ceremonies, constructing and decorating improvised Christmas trees with makeshift ornaments, and even exchanging gifts. Some other men translated the ceremonies of Christmas into their seagoing setting through songs or art work.

Regardless of where the ships were, ships' cooks did their best to make holidays festive. They prepared special menus with roast turkey or other treats. Artists in the crews and the Yeomen combined their drawing and typing skills to print festive looking holiday dinner menus and posted them on bulletin boards. One such menu is shown here.

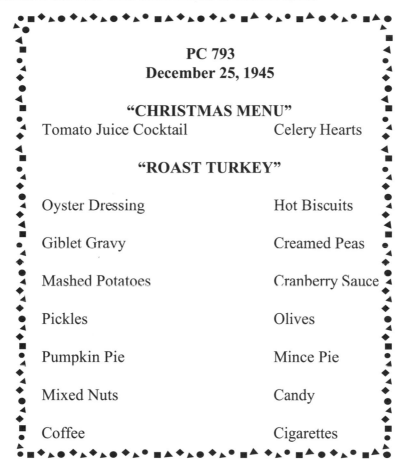

PC 793
December 25, 1945

"CHRISTMAS MENU"

Tomato Juice Cocktail	Celery Hearts

"ROAST TURKEY"

Oyster Dressing	Hot Biscuits
Giblet Gravy	Creamed Peas
Mashed Potatoes	Cranberry Sauce
Pickles	Olives
Pumpkin Pie	Mince Pie
Mixed Nuts	Candy
Coffee	Cigarettes

Figure IV-14. The figure above is a menu for Christmas dinner on 25 December 1945 on PC 793. It is From the author's collection.

Americans loved to celebrate their Independence Day on the fourth of July with displays of fire works. During the war they did little of that Stateside because of the need to save gun powder for munitions. Overseas, service men generally saw enough real life fireworks not to bother with artificial firework displays, and they could be misread as enemy attacks. This fact was certainly true for small ship sailors. Some, however, did acknowledge the day with at least a festive meal. A ship's menu for one of those Fourth of July days is displayed here.

Figure IV-15. The front cover of the folded menu shows a Chief who enjoyed the Cook's preparations for the Fourth of July and a sailor about to arouse him. The menu was from the Antisubmarine School at Key West, Florida. The picture was from Richard Reynold's collection. It is courtesy of his son, Rick Reynolds.

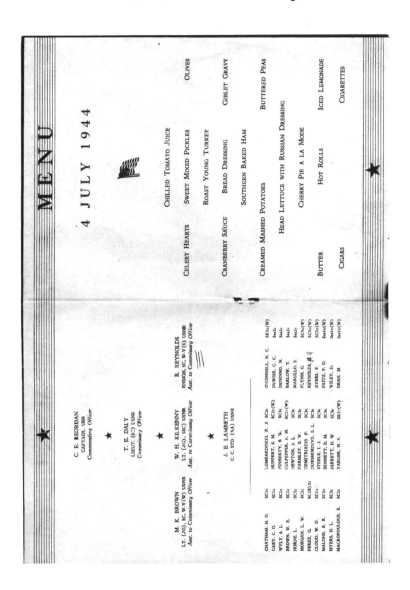

Figure IV-16. This figure shows the inside of the Fourth of July menu whose outside cover is shown in the figure above this one. It is courtesy of Rick Reynolds.

Menus always included cigarettes as the last item. During the war, especially aboard ship, a cigarette was the traditional way to end a meal. Cigarettes also were an important part of most men's lives. Most sailors smoked, day and night wherever and whenever they could. But aboard ship they could not smoke at all times and in all places, only when an order was given that, "The Smoking Lamp is Lit." Regardless of when and where smoking was allowed the ashes and butts had to be disposed of properly for safety and for cleanliness. An ash tray was the proper receptacle to use, but the Navy did not provide them on ships. Sailors overcame this lack of ash trays by making their own. Many men sawed off the base of a spent 3"-50 gun round, smoothed the cut edge, and plunked it down on a desk, bench, or other surface. Other men added refinements.

Figure IV-17. This ash tray made from a 3"-50 shell was embellished with bent coins for cigarette holders and is stamped with USS PC 615. On the other side is stamped, "Lt Herbert Katzenberg, USNR." The lieutenant made this tray while on convoy duty between New York, Guantanamo and Trinidad. The photograph is courtesy of Herbert Katzenberg.

Similarly to other holidays sailors celebrated New Year's Day as best they could depending on their duty and the circumstances of war. Cooks worked hard on that occasion to give the men a different meal from their usual fare, and often there was an artist to decorate the menu. These menus, when posted, were read by the crew with great anticipation of their special meal.

Figure IV-18. This is the cover on a menu for New Year's Day 1945. It shows one hung-over sailor with a head as big as his ship and two others, the old year and the new year, who also wished they had drunk fewer cans of three-two beer or other alcohol they had sneaked aboard ship. Norm Helford drew the picture. It is courtesy of Donald F. Townsend.

Many small ships were engaged in convoy, escort, and transport duties between places where the crews could take liberty and see other countries. While there they saw other military installations and observed the customs and dress of other peoples. Some impressions of the observations of other countries by one sailor are given in the following four figures. They are black and white renditions of water colors which are shown in the Section titled Color Plates.

Figure IV-19. This black and white copy of a water color painting shows a French Army Base at Tenes, Tunisia in N. W. Africa in May 1943. The water color was by and is courtesy of George Amaral.

Figure IV-20. This water color was made of a dancer in N. W. Africa in 1944. Note also the Arab man wearing a flat top cap with a tassel. The painting was by and is courtesy of George Amaral.

Figure IV-21. This interpretation of a Sheik in N. W. Africa in 1944 shows a regal style of dress. The water color was by and is courtesy of George Amaral.

Figure IV-22. The Muslim woman in N. W. Africa shown in this water color wearing a burqha or hijab was made in 1944. Note the Minaret in the background. The painting was by and is courtesy of George Amaral.

Clothing worn by Muslim women did not please the moods or desires of American sailors as shown in the following cartoon.

Figure IV-23. This cartoon shows how sailors appreciated the dress of women in the USA with a "Very Goot, Joe, Yes," as the Arabs would say and a "No Goot Joe," as the Yanks would say about the attire of Arab women. This cartoon was in <u>The Daily Blow</u> a ship's paper on PC 546, Sunday, September 19, 1943. It is courtesy of George Amaral.

Next to "mail call" and liberty ashore what sailors enjoyed most was getting promoted. Promotions to higher rate or rank meant more pay and privileges, but more important was recognition for their accomplishments and loyal duty. Usually some sort of celebration or "wetting down" at the local beer hall or officer's club accompanied a man's promotion. Then too, there were artists who rendered the occasion in a permanent impression.

CHIEF SIDEBOTTOM AT THE HELM.

Figure IV-24. In this cartoon Frank O. Gustafson, an engineer on PC 1132, recorded, with good natured humor, the promotion of Ed Sidebottom to Chief Motor Machinist Mate (CMoMM) in 1945. He took artistic liberty by making a MoMM a right arm rate[13] and having him man the helm instead of the engines.

Life on a small ship in World War II had many aspects similar to those on any ship, but it also had its particular characteristics. And these characteristics were similar to those on any of the small ships. Because of the small size of their steel or wood homes, commissioned officers and enlisted men lived in a crowded space. They were always in contact with each other, often in physical contact. They learned about each other's past, likes and dislikes, and desires. From this knowledge they developed close and lasting friendships. The poem given here expresses their friendly association because of that knowledge.

OLD SIDEBOTTOM

Now old Si was an Engineer
And a good engineer was he.
But he has some faults; one
Is he drinks too Damn Much Beer.

Now old Si was a Gambling Fool
As you can plainly see.
He spends his money when he is in port
And loses out to sea.

He is a Mighty Fellow; From
Oklahoma too.
As you see there is no chance
To tell him what to do.

Frank O. Gustafson wrote this poem while on PC 1132. It is courtesy of Ed Sidebottom.

The majority of crew members on these ships were fresh from civilian life, Reservists, not Regular Navy. Because of this background they were not imbued with the traditions of naval life or big ship procedures, and they were not interested in a naval career. Therefore, military discipline on small ships tended to be somewhat relaxed, and the relationships between officers and men, though disciplined, was amicable. Also, crew members could visit, examine, stand watches in, and work in all of the ships' compartments and areas. They got to know every part of their ships. They knew the size, the shape, the sounds, the motions of every place on the ships. These sensations they would always recall.

Though most sailors joined the naval service reluctantly they knew they should serve their country, and they did their duty to help fight the war thrust upon the United States in 1941. In many cases men would have preferred duty aboard a large ship, but it was not their choice. The Navy chose to send some sailors to small ships, to the Donald Duck Navy.

Once aboard their new small craft they discovered how difficult it was to be a small ship sailor, and they soon developed pride in their service. Despite their pride, though, they still recognized and complained about the difficult conditions of their small steel or wood "home," the frustration of not having personal freedom, and the rigors of life at sea. They moaned, complained, and bitched about their ship, the conditions on board, the duty they performed, the officers, and all that separated them from homes, families, and friends.

Regardless of their conditions, problems, and sacrifices, however, they maintained their good nature, high spirits, and humor, and they displayed it in many original and artistic ways. Some of those expressions are collected in this chapter and elsewhere in this book.

CHAPTER V

PC PATROL CRAFT

The PC Patrol Craft were among the first newly constructed antisubmarine vessels to enter the Battle of the Atlantic after the United States declared war on the Axis Powers.[14] Of the 361 PC hulls built at sixteen shipyards in the United States they were of four classes designated PC 451, PC 452, PC 461, and PC 1586 class. Of them, PC 461 was the most numerous class. Two photograph of and specifications for a typical PC are in Appendix B and Appendix C.

The control ship, PCC, types were of the same hull design and general configuration except for additional electronic gear, armament, and crew complement. The Navy converted some PCs to motor gun boats, PGMs, and mine sweepers, AMs. The PGM type had additional armor and armament. The AM type had mine sweeping gear, and some conversions used different engines. Photographs and specifications for these ships also are given in Appendix B and Appendix C.

Approximately 40,000 men served on these ships during World War II in every theater of war. Foreign navies received some ships during and after the war.[15] Some of the crews of the countries that received the ships during the war trained at places like the Subchaser Training Center in Miami. Many of the ships continued to serve the United States Navy and other navies for decades after the war in places around the world and in various conflicts and peace time roles.

When wartime conditions and censorship permitted, the United States Navy and Coast Guard and many crew members took photographs of their ships. Many of the photographs are in the public domain such as the National Archives and the Navy Department. Others are in books including those cited in the Notes, the Bibliography, and the Related Websites in this book.

Countless other photographs of the ships and their crews remain in personal collections, many of which have not been widely displayed. Those personal collections are not only a grand source of memories but a treasure trove of historic information.

In addition to photographs, some sailors made sketches and paintings of their ships and of other ships with which they operated. These renditions capture not only the overall design and details, but also the artists' feelings for the spirit and uniqueness, of these ships. Like the photographs these drawings and paintings also are of historic importance.

Six of these paintings, given on the next three pages in black and white, show many details of PCs and their surroundings as interpreted by three sailor artists.

Figure V-1. This is a black and white copy of a painting of PC 543 in drydock at La Goulette, Tunisia in 1943. The painting was by and is courtesy of Robert Baldwin.

Figure V-2. This is a black and white copy of a painting of PC 543 moored with two other PCs at the Advanced Amphibious Training Base (AATB) in Bizerte, Tunisia in July 1943. The painting was by and is courtesy of Robert Baldwin.

Figure V-3. Here the artist shows PC 543 entering Termini Imerese harbor on the north coast of Sicily in 1943. Note the local craft in the background. The painting was by and is courtesy of Robert Baldwin.

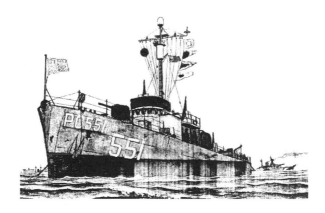

Figure V-4. This is a painting of PC 551 anchored off Bizerte, Tunisia, circa 1943. Note the British Monitor standing out to sea at the right and the masts of a sunken Italian freighter at the left. The ball on the yardarm is the "anchor" ball. The painting was by and is courtesy of Robert Baldwin.

Figure V-5. This black and white rendition is of a color painting made by Sid Frey of PC 616. It shows PC 616, accompanied by another escort ship and flying uncle, victor, king, oboe, mike, fox from her signal halyards. It was in the collection of Richard Reynolds of PC 616. It is courtesy of Rich Reynolds. The painting in color is in the Section of this book titled Color Plates.

Figure V-6. This sketch shows PC 1122 underway in a moderate sea. Note that the guns are uncovered and the gun crews are standing by as the ship probably anticipates action. The drawing was made by and is courtesy of William (Bill) Buffington.

Men who served on PCs knew their ships as rugged and rough riders. They lurched and swivelled so viciously that they taxed a man's patience, endurance, fortitude, and strength. PC Sailors complained and "bitched" about their ships. The men aboard had no privacy. They had only Spartan accommodations that allowed little comfort and were crowded, damp, cold or hot, noisy, and rough riding. But most men who served on them had an affection for them and were proud to be on them. The following poem distills some of the love-hate relationship these sailors had for their ships, and it expresses the pride they took in being a PC sailor.

THE PC BOAT

Can you sit serene on a broncho mean,
Or stay on a plunging steer?
Can you calmly flop in a boiler shop
And peacefully pound your ear?
Can you keep your feet on freezing sleet
In a wind that'll chill you through?
Then maybe, mate, you've the stuff to rate
A berth with a PC crew.
Swoop like a gull, dive like a plover,
Turn on a dime with a nickel over,
Racing whippet and jumping goat –
Leaping Lena, the PC boat.

Melvin DeWitt, Signalman on PC564 wrote and contributed this poem about a "broncho (sic) mean."

Life on a PC was not always exciting, dangerous, and filled with action. Much of the time the duty was routine and even boring. This was especially true on submarine patrol, picket duty, and convoy duty while protecting merchant ships from German U-boats and Italian and Japanese submarines. During some of their idle hours off watch and secured from General Quarters men slept, relaxed, read and wrote letters, or joined in Scuttlebutt. Some, however, became more actively engaged and recorded the design and details of their ships and shipmates with pencil or ink on paper. The following figure shows one such drawing.

Figure V-7. This view looks aft in the mess hall on a PC. It shows the entrance ladder with the water cooler to its right (starboard) when descending. To its left (port) are the hatch to the galley and the coffee urn. Also shown is a bunk triced up and a mess hall table littered with personal items belonging to the crew. The drawing was made by Bob Baldwin in 1943 on PC 1181.

In addition to the many drawings and paintings he made, Bob Baldwin also climbed around and crawled through all of the decks and compartments on the ship on which he served, PC 543. In his off duty hours he roamed the decks fore and aft and port to starboard observing all the items on the decks from the anchors to the depth charge racks.

He wandered through the wheel house studying the helm, voice tube, sound gear, annunciator, and all else. He recorded every thing in the flying bridge, the chart room, the radar shack, the radio area, the Yeoman's section, and the ward room. Topside, he studied the guns, the flag bag, and other parts on the weather decks. Bob even climbed the mast to the crow's nest to record the rigging and get an overall view of the ship.

While climbing and roaming about the ship, he examined every part of PC 543. When he did this, he carried with him a tape measure, a pencil, and paper, and he measured items and sketched overviews and most of the details of his ship from the largest items right down to the sizes of nuts and bolts. He recorded all but the engine room. Four of the rough drawings he made at that time are shown on the next four pages.

After leaving the Navy Bob Baldwin converted his rough sketches into thirty engineering drawings he called Plates. They are some of the most complete, accurate, and detailed renditions of PCs available today. All thirty of his plates are shown in the Section titled Plates – Engineering Drawings of a PC. Though they are for a PC they are much like the gear and the layout of compartments on other small ships.

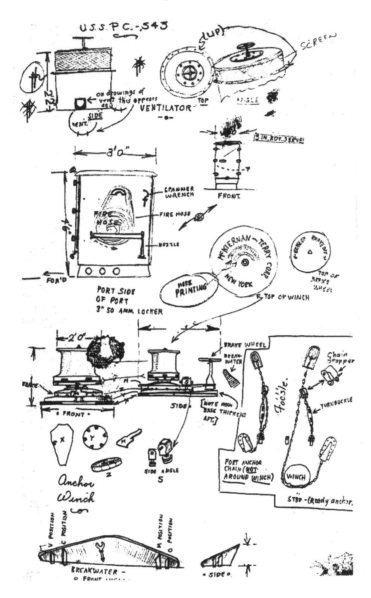

Figure V-8. This sketch shows details of items on the forecastle of PC 543. It is by and courtesy of Bob Baldwin.

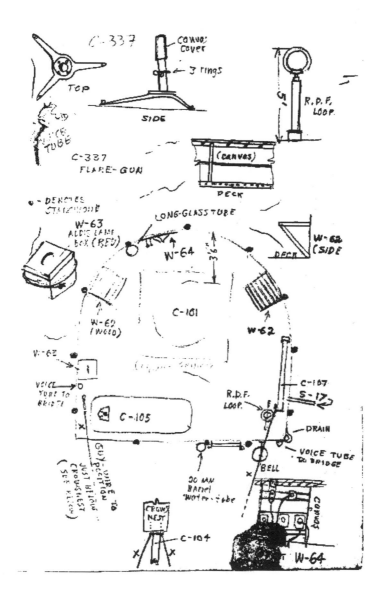

Figure V-9. In this drawing Bob shows details of other items on the deck. The drawing is by and courtesy of Bob Baldwin.

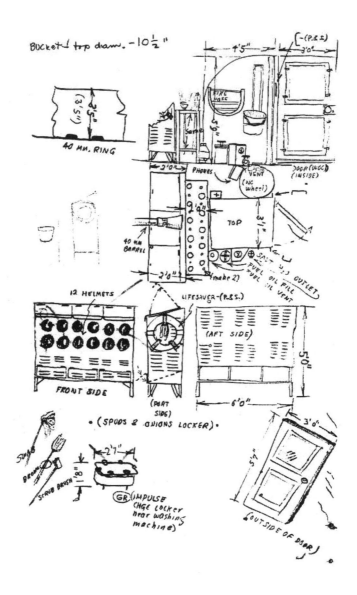

Figure V-10. Here Bob shows items on the flying bridge and elsewhere. The drawing is by and courtesy of Bob Baldwin.

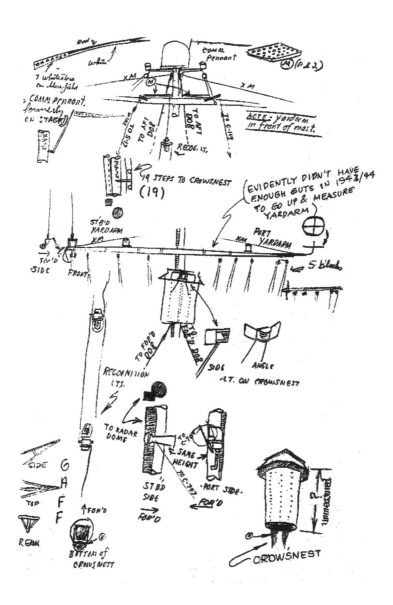

Figure V-11. This sketch shows some details of the mast and crows nest. The drawing is by and courtesy of Bob Baldwin.

Despite the uncomfortable, rugged, dangerous, and often boring life on a small ship, the men accepted their life, joked about it, and took pride in their efforts. The following poem sums up much of that life.

THIS LIFE WE LEAD

Strike up the ensign
and run up the jack.
Heave on the lines
and take in the slack.

Wash down the deck
and pick up the ship.
Where salt lies heavy
from our twenty day trip.

Lay up to the wardroom
and fall in for play.
No stutter or fuss,
get things underway.

Then pass out the mail
for fear it won't keep.
Open her letter,
read it and weep!

Three bells and a jingle,
the liberty boat waits.
We're going ashore
and pick up some dates.

> That's the routine life
> a sailor must see.
> In convoy duty
> on a damn PC!

This poem is presented here with the courtesy of Marvin D. Polin. It was printed in the PCSA Newsletter, No. 23, Jan. – March 1994.

As stated in the poem:
> "the liberty boat waits.
> We're going ashore
> and pick up some dates."

And of course that was what sailors always looked forward to doing. Liberty was a chance to leave the ship, walk the land, see the sights, have a drink, and look for women. When on liberty in the United States sailors got along quite well with all the people. There, the way of life and the language was familiar, and they understood the customs. Then too, during World War II, the spirit of patriotism and respect for what servicemen were doing made people, including young women, at home willing and anxious to help and to entertain sailors.

While sailors were away from the States, however, they experienced concern that the young men who were still at home, especially those zootsuiters, might be dating their girl friends, fiances, and wives. They understood because many of them, before joining the service, had worn pegged pants, dangled long key chains, had Duck's Ass haircuts, and had chased the ladies. This thought nagged many of the men. One sailor showed his concern about the safety and faithfulness of his girl back home in the paintings shown in the following two Figures.

Figure V-12. This black and white copy of a painting depicts a typical "zootsuiter" of the early 1940s. Many men who went into the Navy showed up at Boot Camp dressed like the man in the figure. The painting was made by Robert S. Laurie and was made available by Clyde Dauben. Both men served on PC 478. The painting in color is in the Section of this book titled Color Plates.

Figure V-13. In this black and white copy of the painting of an invitation to a dance by a zootsuiter, the caption warns, "Watch out for Any Sailors." The painting was by Robert S. Laurie and was made available by Clyde Dauben. The painting in color is in the Section of this book titled Color Plates.

Liberty in overseas ports was different from that in the States because of unfamiliar customs and language barriers in other countries. In most cases that did not deter sailors, though, and they seemed to get along quite well and even, as written in the poem given above, "pick up some dates." A typical liberty scene in Tunis, Africa is shown in the Figure on this page.

Figure V-14. This black and white image shows the USO in Tunis, N. W. Africa in 1943. The water color was made by and is courtesy of George Amaral, SK 2/C, who served on PC 546. The painting in color is in the Section of this book titled Color Plates.

When Imperial Japan brought the war to the United States many young men volunteered for or were selected for duty in the United States Naval and Coast Guard Reserves. They entered the Navy and Coast Guard and accepted the obligation and need to defeat the aggressors. The Navy trained a group of them and assigned them to the PC type of subchasers. These men not only made the best of their assignment, they became eager to prove their ships and themselves. The determination of those young men who served on PCs, for example, is displayed in the following poem.

A PC POEM

From the great Pacific Ocean,
   to the Island of Japan,
We've a score to settle,
   and the time is now at hand.
We're gonna build some PC's,
   and sail them across the sea.
For the people of America,
   they love democracy.
Hear the mighty PC engines,
   hear the angry bullets whine.
We are going to use them,
   to eliminate the swine.
There'll be peace forever,
   on that far and distant land.
When you see a PC patrolling,
   'round the Island of Japan.

This poem was composed in 1943 by K. J. Schwartz who served on PC1125. It is courtesy of K. J. Schwartz.

During off watch hours some men passed the time with handcrafts including making knife handles, ashtrays, belt buckles, and jewelry. A few men made ships models, but usually not of the ships on which they served. This was because wartime censorship did not permit them to send home replicas of naval craft for fear the enemy might intercept them and learn ships' details. Some men were more persistent and clever, however, and avoided the censorship restrictions. They were wrong then to violate censorship rules, but now we are happy that they did. These replicas of PCs are all that one can use to visualize the ships that no longer exist. One unique model of a PC made by a man who served aboard one is shown in the three photographs below.

Figure V-15. Harry Burry, a young Lieutenant on PC 563, made this model of his ship during 1943-44. He gave the model to his bride as a first wedding anniversary present in March 1944. The scale of the model is 1:100, and the model is approximately twenty-one inches long. The unique feature is that Lt. Burry carved the model from a single block of pine. The photographs of the model and information about it are courtesy of Peter Lessing.

In addition to making belt buckles, ash trays, jewelry, and other items, a favorite hand craft was knife handles. Often men stripped the handle from a knife and built a handle of their own expressing their personal taste. One unique knife handle, however, was installed on the blade of a Japanese bayonet.

In 1944 sailors from PC 1132 brought back to the ship a broken point of a Japanese bayonet they found on New Guinea. Ed Sidebottom ground, filed, and threaded part of the bayonet to fit a handle. He drilled and filed a brass plate to form the handle stop at the dagger end. Ed drilled pieces of leather and stacked and fitted them over the handle. Next he drilled and tapped a block of aluminum, and screwed it down over the stacked leathers. Then he sawed, ground, filed, shaved, and polished the handle and the blade. A photograph of the finished dagger is shown here.

Figure V-16. This photograph is of a dagger made by Ed Sidebottom in 1944. It was made from a broken Japanese bayonet found on New Guinea. The photograph is courtesy of Ed Sidebottom.

The United States Navy had sixteen shipyards build 361 ships on PC hulls. Most of the ships remained as standard PCs, but the Navy converted some to minesweepers and gun boats.[16] The PCs were among the first ships to do battle with the Nazi U-boats after the United States entered World War II. From there they went on to serve in all theaters of war.

Typically PCs had crews of sixty enlisted men and five commissioned officers. With transfers and replacements there may have been about one hundred men to serve on a PC. This resulted in almost 40,000 men who went to sea on them.

Among those young men were many who made original contributions to music, writing, art, handcrafts, and modeling. Much of it is still in private collections and memoirs. This chapter includes only a sample of their work, but it illustrates their outstanding creativity and the range of their work despite the difficult lives they led.

CHAPTER VI

SC SUBMARINE CHASERS

Shortly after the United States entered the Battle of the Atlantic against the Nazi U-boats, the Navy of the United States sent to sea the new wooden hull submarine chasers designated SC.[17] During World War II the Navy commissioned 438 of these little ships and sent them on missions similar to and as varied and dangerous as those of any of the other type of subchaser or small ship. Smaller and lighter than most other ships and made from wood, these vessels tossed on the seas as much or more than any of the other small ships. For their crews life aboard them was more crowded and uncomfortable than on almost any ship of the Donald Duck Navy. The young men who sailed SCs truly upheld the old seagoing tradition of iron men on wooden ships. A photograph of an SC is shown in Appendix B, and a color picture of one is in the Section titled Color Plates.

The SC was among the smallest of the ocean going ships, and because of their shallow draft and narrow beam the sea tossed them about like corks. A number of their crew members recorded their life aboard such as in the following poem.

TO THE SC

Hail to thee, rolling scow,
Ship thou never wer't
That from hell or farther below,
Plungest thy wet bow
In the ocean's every trough.

Higher still, and higher
On the wave's crest. thou lingerest
Like a ping pong ball;
Into the blue sea, thou plungest
And tossing still dost roll
And rolling ever tosseth.

Never a moment's peace thou giveth
On the ocean's blue;
Like the soul of a judas
It seems you are troubled too;
By what, I cannot tell,
Unless you are giving us
A coming attraction of hell.

Fie on you, vicious thing
In your mad desire to give us a fling
Upon the unyielding oaken deck.
Dost thou not know
You might break our neck?

Alas, you care naught
For a berth in port,
For you would rather be
A'searching for a rougher sea;
So much like a debauchee

Looking forward to a mad spree.
But e'en though, I curse you like I do
Until my face is blue;
In my heart there is a tender spot
But I'll be damned if it is for you!

This poem is courtesy of Dick Sloane of SC 739 and Ted Treadwell.

Another poem by an SC sailor also lyrically describes the rough ride on an SC at sea.

ABOARD THIS OLD SC

Have you ever stood on the flying bridge
With the spray going over your head?
When you try to sleep in your sack at night
You bounce to the overhead.

When chow is called in the morning,
Believe me it is no thrill
To sit down to a cup of java
When the darn thing won't sit still.

The way she pitches and tosses
Makes your head go round and round;
You go hang over the fantail
While your belly turns upside down.

I suppose you think I'm talking
Of some storm far out to sea;
To you battleship sailors it would be calm
But it's not when you're on an SC

No don't think I'm complaining
Or that I want to squawk,
But believe me, mate, if I had my way
I'd darn sight rather walk.

So as you sail on smoothly
Please give a thought to me;
I'll still be getting tossed around
Aboard this old SC.

This poem was written by H. Finneran. It is courtesy of Ted Treadwell.

SC sailors took pride in serving on one of the navy's smallest type warship, and they decorated their ships with humorous or aggressive insignia such as the one shown in Chapter II and the figure on the next page.

Figure VI-1. This sketch of Bugs Bunny was painted on a
sheet of plywood and displayed on the flying bridge of SC 980 in
1945. Bugs Bunny was chosen because of the frequent comment by
crew members, "What's up Doc?" a famous remark by Bugs Bunny.
Seaman 1/C Culp is the man in the picture. The figure was drawn by
and is courtesy of Richard Elmendorf.

SC sailors suffered the same indignity suffered by all
small ship sailors in that the Navy, news media, and historians
tended to ignore them and their accomplishments. Despite this
lack of recognition, the men who served on them maintained
their dignity and understood their contributions to winning
World War II. Some of this attitude is summed up in the
following poem.

THE SPLINTER FLEET

They sing the praises of the battleship,
The carrier is queen of the sea,
The cruiser is tops on the sailor's lists
For a fighting ship is she.

The destroyer sails the sea with pride,
The submarine's work is neat,
But we are the legion of forgotten men,
The sailors in the SC fleet.

We are indeed a motherless child,
A long, long way from home.
Our base is any port we make,
For our destiny is to roam.

No concern is shown for the work we do,
No thought for the way we live,
Like sardines we're packed in wooden crates
Which usually leak like a sieve.

We bounce around like a piece of cork,
No rest is to be had at sea,
The duty is tough and never ends
But the life we live is free.

Our chow all comes from a box or can,
Nothing fresh ever comes this way.
We do our laundry in the propeller wash,
It's a system that's here to stay.

We comb our hair with a ki-yi brush,
Take showers in the water from the sea,
Our trademark is ruggedness,
Yes, a salty bunch are we.

Our stay in port is never long,
For we have work to do,
We have forgotten the comforts of civilian
 life,
And are happy where the water is blue.

Wooden ships with iron men,
Is a tradition centuries old,
We live up to that in the Splinter Fleet,
When on convoy and patrol.

Our purpose is like the Concord light,
A continuous vigil at sea,
Protecting ships from submarines,
To keep our country free.

Theodore R. (Ted) Treadwell, Skipper of SC 648, wrote, in his book titled, *Splinter Fleet*, that Oris E. Moore, a Gunner's Mate on SC 1016, while on duty in the Caribbean, in 1942 sat on an ammunition ready box and scribbled this poem on a yellow legal pad.

Sailors who served on these wooden ships knew they were a special group who endured hardships not experienced by big ship sailors. They were proud to let other Navy men know which ship they served on as shown by the following figure of an SC emblazoned on the back of a Navy issue corduroy jacket.

Figure VI-2. This silhouette of SC 980 was drawn on a foul weather jacket at Charleston, South Carolina while waiting for the ship to be commissioned. The jacket is still preserved by Richard Elmendorf who drew the picture. The photograph is courtesy of Richard Elmendorf.

Officers held inspections frequently, and the men worked hard at keeping their ships clean. But because of the constant shipping of water at sea and rain seeping into the spaces, moisture in the compartments was always a problem. Add to that issue tropical temperatures and the difficulty of handling and serving food. These conditions made SCs ripe for having uninvited and unwelcome stowaways aboard. That problem is summed up in the following poem.

HI'YA COCKROACH!

T'rou' da bilges went da cockroach,
t'rou' da bilges, t'rou' da galley.
Found day food and found day feasting,
t'rou' da galley, t'rou' da lockers,
'Til we catchem wid da Flit gun,
den day take da Flit gun from us,
Move us over at da table,
holler "Guts!" and pound da table,
Claim day cannot eat dat moose dung!
So went sailors t'rou' da bilges,
T'rou' da bilges, t'rou da galley.
Locked demselves inside da lockers,
Barricade demselves wid broomsticks,
Lived on scraps da bugs would t'row dem,
While da cockroach, unmolested,
Took command and gave da orders,
and da Navy was no wiser.
So at night we roam da bilges.
T'rou' da bilges, t'rou' da galley,
And at night you hear us scratching,
t'rou' da bilges, t'rou' da galley.

Al Angelini, Pharmacists Mate on SC 744, found this poem, that exalted the lowly cockroach, among papers of Yeoman, Robert F. Maire, transferred off SC 744. Angelini sent it to Theodore R. Treadwell who quoted it in his book. It is not known if Maire wrote it or got it from another source. Regardless of the author's name, it is the product of and illustrates one of the dilemmas of being a small ship sailor.

Not all the sailors' observations were frivolous or lighthearted. These men on the small ships saw and were part of the bedlam and death of war. Many times small ships, such as SCs led the landing craft to invasion beaches. There they saw, contributed to, and suffered the consequences of battle. Their experiences moved the men emotionally in many ways. One such reminiscence is expressed in the following poem.

OFF THE BEACH AT AITAPE

Close your eyes, old man. Listen.
Hear the hiss of bow through slicksmooth water.
Smell the swamp mist, smell the damp rot,
Smell the stale sweat of 3,000 sons at dawn.
Off the beach at Aitape.

Tremble in the chill air, old man.
Shove dryspit down your throat.
Suck in the roar. Listen.
Hear the death raining down
On the beach at Aitape.

Open your eyes old man. Look.
See the butchery where once
Was the beach at Aitape.

Ted Treadwell wrote of his moment of inspiration for this poem during the invasion of Aitape, "Some moments etch themselves deeply within the subconscious. Minute details – the smell, the quiet, the gray, the damp, the chill – stay with you forever. H-hour at Aitape was just such a moment for me."

Ted Treadwell added another somber thought to his duty on an SC when he wrote in the dedication of his book *Splinter Fleet:*[18]

"To the brave young men who served in the Splinter Fleet – and especially those who did not return

"Though shattered planks 'neath oceans lie,
Their souls in peace shall never die."

Wooden ships have been in the Navy and Coast Guard of the United States since their inception. By the 20th century, however, steel ships replaced most wooden men-of-war and Cutters. Wooden naval ships became fewer in number and assumed fewer of the fighting duties of the Navy. Sailors mourned their passing, and historians liberally accumulated and wrote about their history.

When the United States entered World War I they rejuvenated the idea of wooden ships as subchasers labeled SCs. Though they achieved minor success, the idea was reborn for World War II. Eventually the Navy built 438 of these ships for World War II and manned them with Navy and Coast Guard crews. They played a major role in the war not only as subchasers but as beach control vessels, escorts, and in various other ways.

The young men, mostly Reservists, who served on them took pride in their duty and displayed it where they could as shown in the samples in this chapter.

CHAPTER VII

OTHER SMALL SHIPS

Among the small ships of the United States Navy and Coast Guard there were more PCs and SCs than the other types listed in the Introduction. It is expected then that not as much original material, such as in this book, would be available from the sailors of other ships as is available from the men who served on the PC and SC type ships.

However, some of the material that was generated by sailors from these ships other than PCs and SCs has been discovered and was contributed by the originators for inclusion in this book. It is shown in this chapter.

Appendix B and Appendix C contain photographs and specifications of the other small ships listed in the Introduction..

The men who served on these various subchaser and minesweeper ships, took great pride in their service and their special status. They considered themselves a particular type of sailor who was ready for any hazardous duty anywhere. They were rugged. They were tenacious. And, as shown in the cartoon on the next page, they were Nasty.

Figure VII-1. "I'm Nasty Naturally . . . I'm a Sub Chaser!!!" This drawing by and courtesy of Bill Buffington shows the attitude of subchaser sailors toward the enemy.

The majority of crew members on these ships were fresh from civilian life, not long out of Boot Camp. They still showed their lack of Navy protocol and procedures as suggested in the following cartoon of a man in Boot Camp.

Figure VII-2. This rendition is of a recruit (Boot) at the Great Lakes Naval Training Center who followed the axiom to salute almost any one. It was drawn by Lee Barber from PCS 1389.

As on most ships the men in the crew needed diversion from their dreary routines and constant dangers, and they needed reminders of what it was like at home. To help satisfy these needs the men considered holidays, such as Thanksgiving, as special events. Despite their condition, giving thanks that their lives were not worse, the artists aboard and the cooks combined their talents and skills for a festive meal.

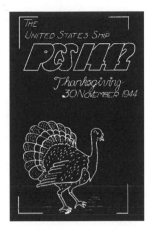

Figure VII-3. This front cover is for a menu for Thanksgiving Day on PCS 1442 in 1944. Robert Lewis, George Chekas, and an unknown artist prepared the menu. It is courtesy of Al Bellanca.

Figure VII-4. This is the back cover for the menu above. It is courtesy of Al Bellanca.

Sailors on YMSs also had their poets to describe the rugged life on those small wooden ships that rode the seas like corks.

AN ODE TO THE YMS

Listen men I've a tale to tell
of mighty ships that sail like — well.
With a word to the wise on larger ships
to forget those small craft transfer slips.

Men don't live on YMSs
They Just exist under strains and stresses.
Tossed around like a bundle of peas
inside their ship on the calmest of seas.

Did you ever eat on a YMS?
It has been done at times, I guess.
But the simplest of meals can come to grief,
when we hit the wake of a passing leaf.

An order came to batten hatches
for days on end we all wore patches.
What dire calamity caused all this?
A passing school of playful fish.

This battered life is just one item.
We've many more, just let me cite 'em,
We scrub our whites – they come back black.
Our clothes line boys is behind the stack.

The spacious locker, I might mention
is always full, and gosh – the tension.
I wish the navy were more lenient,
four rubber walls would be convenient.

When "o two hundred" all's secure,
the old mud hook is deep and sure.
And even though the sea's like granite
she is off to another planet.

Just one more point to end my tale
of little ships and how they sail;
half submarine, the other half plane,
they're a secret weapon gone insane.

Ah, yes, my friend if big ships bore you;
the YMS is waiting for you.
With loving care both fore and aft,
the navy designed them and laughed and laughed.

The author of this poem, circa 1945, is unknown. It is courtesy of J. M. Passmann of YMS 289.

The YMS and PCS types were small ships, but there were even smaller ones. Sailors on them also told their tales and recorded their ships in art work. One illustration of the art work done by sailors on one of the smallest of the small ships, that were used mainly for harbor patrol, the YP, is shown next.

Figure VII-5. This figure is a black and white copy of a painting by James H. Byington of YP 478. A color copy is in the Section titled Color Plates. Property of the Bay County Historical Society, used with permission.

In addition to men painting insignia on their ships, some painted symbols on places like the stack of their ship, that also depicted the ship's purpose and duty. Next is one example of such "stack art."

AUGIE
USS INAUGURAL
AM 242

Figure VII-6. This cartoon sailor is shown with a broom ready to sweep the Japanese mine he holds in his other hand. A color copy is in the Section titled Color Plates. It was from AMA 242 and is courtesy of Jack M. Passmann.

The Navy converted some SCs to gunboats called PGMs. Because they were modifications, or hybrids, they seemed like strange naval craft to some sailors and performed unlikely missions as described in the following poem.

ABOUT PGMS

Our little ship all painted green,
Is the oddest thing I've ever seen.
It is not large, it is not fast,
It has no deck house, it has no mast.
It's guns are small, it's armor naught,
In no great battles has it fought.
Of it's achievements we cannot boast,
As it's life was spent patrolling a coast.
But down in history it's battle cry will go:
"Afire the mortar at three two zero."
Go, cried the captain, we rush pell mell,
To blow our objective to hell.
The gunners are nervous and fidget about,
When the captain gives orders in a loud shout.
Open up with three inch, fifties hold fast,
Now with the forty, thirty sevens last.
Cease firing he cries, secure from go,
I have something to say to you.
I would like to pat each of you on the back,
For behold you've destroyed another grass shack.

This poem was written by Bill Layton on PGM 5 (ex SC 1056). It is courtesy of Ted Treadwell.

Through their art work and photographs that men took they committed their ships and their shipmates to memory for the future. Though I have not considered, in this book, photographs as a part of the original works of small ship sailors, one sailor produced a photograph in a unique way that shows the creative spirit. The photograph was part of an end of the war souvenir booklet titled "Quarters for Muster" that was presented to members of the crew of PCS 1442.

Figure VII-7. This is the cover of a booklet issued to all crew members of PCS 1442 at the end of World War II. It contains photographs of the ship and the officers and men. Al Bellanca made the booklet. It is courtesy of Al Bellanca.

The collage, from the booklet above, captures and distills what life was like aboard a small ship in World War II so I present it on the following page as a reminder to all small ship sailors of what life was like "aboard."

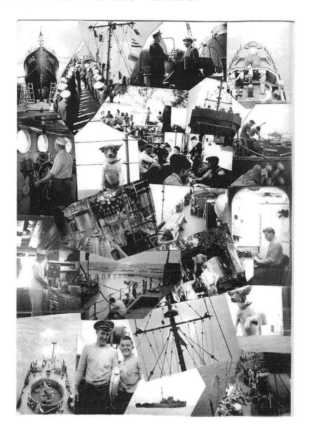

Figure VII-8. This collage of photographs of life aboard a small ship in August 1945 was made by and is courtesy of Al Bellanca.

Large ships of the United States Navy had specific uses and rarely performed missions other than those for which the Navy designed them. With small ships this differed. They frequently got the call to do many and varied tasks, some almost beyond their, and their crews' capabilities. Nonetheless they did their jobs and without fanfare or recognition and acceptance of it as routine.

SONG OF THE YOKE MIKE SUGARS[19]

Our deeds unknown, our banes forgot, but from the States we came,
To sweep through all the channels is our greatest claim to fame,
But anything else that does pop up, we find it's ours to do,
No matter if our screws are bent and we've killed off half our crew.
When we get home to our children, and they ask us what we've done,
Tell them at times we worked a bit but mostly it was fun:
And when they look for medals with their eyes so bright and keen,
Just tell them Daddy hasn't any because it was routine.

These two stanzas are from a poem, the author of which is unknown. It is circa 1945 and is courtesy of Jack M. Passmann.

Life on a small ship in World War II had many aspects similar to those on any ship, but it also had its particular characteristics. The most obvious one was the flexibility and availability of these ships to perform a myriad of different and difficult missions. Their crews accepted this obligation and went about their tasks with professionalism and dignity for which they rarely received any special recognition.

CHAPTER VIII

COAST GUARD

Before 1941, except during earlier wars, the United States Coast Guard was under the Department of the Treasury.[20] But after the United States declared war on the Axis, the Coast Guard became part of the United States Navy, as it always had in time of war. At that time the Coast Guard operated many ships of various types and sizes. Many of them had been built before World War I. Those ships that were built for and during World War II and that, for the purposes of this book, could be considered as small ocean going combat vessels are listed with the number manned by Coast Guard crews. They include[21] Patrol Gunboats, PG (8); Patrol Craft PC (4); Subchasers SC (6). Coast Guard crews also manned pre-war yachts the Navy converted to patrol craft. They included Patrol Vessels, YP (40) and Coastal Yachts PYc (1).

In addition to these ships, the Coast Guard operated numerous other type small vessels and Cutters. Among those that did patrol work are the types WPG, WYP, WPY, WPYc, and WPR. Those considered in this book are the 165' and 125'

Cutters designated Submarine Chaser Large, WPC and Submarine Chaser Small, WSC.

Coast Guard crews, and Coast Guard personnel associated with the Coast Guard, also had among them men with creative talent. They were proud of their contributions to the war and their sharing of dangers with other sailors as illustrated in the following poem.

YOU GOT TO GO OUT, BUT –

From the Coasts of Heaven
To the Coast of Hell,
There's a song they sing,
And a story they tell.

A story of struggle,
A song of sweat,
Of the men who fought,
And are fighting yet.

There were beaches of fire
And beaches of blood,
There was sand and steel,
There was lead and mud.

But the pages of glory
Proclaim the deeds,
That were done by these men.
That the Coast Guard breeds.

They swarmed up the shores
At Guadalcanal.
Behind them was thunder,
Before them was hell.

They piled through the surf
From Algiers to Fedala
They blasted the beach
At Tarawa, at Gela.

And this was their vow
As they led the attack–
"You've got to go out–
You don't have to come back."

The author of this poem is unknown. It appeared on page 14 of the USCG Patrol – For The Tars and Spars of The Boston District, a monthly publication of the U. S. Coast Guard, Boston District, Volume 2, No. 7, June 1944. It is courtesy of Donald F. Townsend.

Like their Navy shipmates, Coast Guard sailors also admired the Donald Duck figure for their ships and stations as embodying some of their spirit. During World War II the Disney Studios drew many logos and insignia for the armed forces including the Coast Guard. The name "Corsair Fleet" was given to Coast Guard craft. One Corsair Fleet emblem is shown in the following figure.

During WW II, Disney Studios produced hundreds of logos for the U.S Armed Forces. The nickname "Corsair Fleet" was given to the thousands of CG and CGR craft that patrolled the coast watching for U-boats and saboteurs. (Courtesy of the National Archives.)

Figure VIII-1. This image was created by the Walt Disney Studios for the Coast Guard, referred to as the Corsair Fleet. A color picture is in the Section titled Color Plates. The image is from and is courtesy of the National Archives.

Coast Guard ships also had insignia painted on their superstructures. Both Navy and Coast Guard sailors admired and took pride in these figures, but some men joked that they made good targets for enemy gunners. One insignia demonstrated that prophecy as shown in the two figures on the next page.

Figure VIII-2. This insignia, painted on the pilot house of a small ship, is being admired by one of the officers. The photograph is unidentified and is from the author's collection.

Figure VIII-3. This photograph shows the figure above after the enemy used it as a target. The photograph is unidentified and is from the author's collection.

Like some Navy Boots, some of those recruits who joined the Coast Guard also had their problems becoming disciplined sailors. The next cartoon depicts one typical problem, close order drill.

Figure VIII-4. This "BONEHEAD"cartoon is from the <u>USCG Patrol – For the Tars and Spars of The Boston District, June 1944.</u> It is courtesy of Donald F. Townsend.

Launching and christening of a ship was always a formal and gala ceremony. Usually it was enhanced by a lady sponsor of the ship who smashed a bottle of champagne on the bow of the vessel. The event did not always go as planned, however, and at times the Coast Guard had problems getting some of their ships launched and christened.

"-OOPS!"

Figure VIII-5. This cartoon of a lady sponsor christening a new Coast Guard ship is from the <u>USCG Patrol – For the Tars and Spars of The Boston District, June 1944.</u> It is courtesy of Donald F. Townsend.

Once the Coast Guard lady sponsors launched their ships, their crews boarded them with enthusiasm and sailed them with intrepid style.

After being land-locked for three months because of repairs, the crew of Flotilla #407, Cambridge, Mass., go out to sea again. A bit proudly, the boys manned their stations as the boat headed for the open harbor. Maybe they could get a sea gull to give them a tow.

Figure VIII-6. This cartoon, depicting Coast Guard men from Flotilla #407 departing Cambridge, Massachusetts so eager to get to sea they raise havoc in the harbor, is from the USCG Patrol – For The Tars and Spars of The Boston District, June 1944. It is courtesy of Donald F. Townsend.

Of course the commissioned officers on board Coast Guard ships sometimes had problems with sailors who, instead of following regulation procedures in which they had been trained, used their ingenuity when operating the ship's helm. A case is shown in the figure on the following page.

No Sir. I don't have any more trouble keeping the needle on the lubber's line since I put magnet there, sir!

Figure VIII-7. This cartoon of a sailor who used a magnet to aid in following the lubber's line is from the <u>USCG Patrol – For The Tars and Spars of The Boston District, June 1944.</u> It is courtesy of Donald F. Townsend.

Ships manned by United States Coast Guard sailors served in all theaters of the war, and like all small ship sailors their uniforms did not always meet big ship standards. Officers frequently relaxed the regulations for the crews and for themselves. Men's ingenuity soon adapted their uniforms to meet the needs of their environment as shown in the following South Pacific Fashion Trends.

Figure VIII-8. This set of drawings, whose author is unknown, shows informal Coast Guard uniform trends in the South Pacific. It is courtesy of Donald F. Townsend.

Coast Guard Tars and Spars (women Coast Guard members) expressed their humor about Spars serving on Shore Patrol (SP) duty, unofficial promotions to impress their girl friends, artistic buglers, and old salts who have been around learning "what it's all about." These ideas are shown in the following four figures.

Figure VIII-9. The Coast Guard had female SPs too. This cartoon is from the <u>USCG Patrol – For The Tars and Spars of The Boston District, June 1944.</u> It was drawn by Norman Samaha. The figure is courtesy of Donald F. Townsend.

Figure VIII-10. This Coast Guard sailor asks his shipmate, "Now don't give me away. She thinks I've been promoted." This cartoon is from the USCG Patrol – For The Tars and Spars of The Boston District, June 1944. It was drawn by Norman Samaha. The figure is courtesy of Donald F. Townsend.

Figure VIII-11. This sailor got some brig time for improvisations on the bugle at reveille. This cartoon is from the <u>USCG Patrol – For The Tars and Spars of The Boston District, June 1944.</u> It was drawn by Norman Samaha. The figure is courtesy of Donald F. Townsend.

Figure VIII-12. A theater door man suggests that two salty, combat veteran sailors learn about war from Hollywood movies. Their Sea Bags provide memories of, "What it's all about." This cartoon is from the USCG Patrol – For The Tars and Spars of The Boston District, June 1944. It was drawn by Norman Samaha. The figure is courtesy of Donald F. Townsend.

With the large number of small ships like PCs, SCs, and Cutters manned by Coast Guard crews, the number of Coast Guard sailors involved in World War II is equivalent to those on the Navy subchaser and minesweeper fleet. These Coast Guard men lived up to their motto "Semper Peratis" in all their actions and on all their ships. They sailed and fought in every theater of the war and contributed equally to both the war effort and to the works of art and humor that American sailors generated during and after World War II.

CHAPTER IX

EXPLOITS ACTIONS AND LOSSES

Ships of the Donald Duck Navy, including those crewed by Coast Guard men, contributed in many ways to the success of the naval war against the Axis powers. They did this in the early days of the entry of the United States in World War II by escorting convoys along the U-Boat infested coast of the Americas. Later they performed the same tasks in every ocean. They also patrolled for and engaged submarines and surface vessels in all the war zones. Their crews fought off and shot down enemy aircraft. They did picket duty along routes aircraft flew to rescue downed airmen. They swept mines in harbors and at invasion beaches around the world.

As World War II progressed, some of the ships led landing craft to most of the invasion beaches in the Mediterranean, Atlantic, and Pacific. And their crews pulled many civilians, merchant men, sailors, and soldiers from the sea saving their lives.

In addition to these well identified tasks the ships and their crews performed many other miscellaneous functions that could be done only by small shallow draft ships with appreciable armament, antisubmarine weapons, or mine sweeping gear. Many of these tasks were undreamed of when the ships were designed, constructed, and sent to sea.

While engaged in these many and varied duties the crews of these ships manned their guns and depth charge stations. They blasted German, Italian, and Japanese aircraft from the skies, depth-charged submarines to the bottom of the sea, damaged and sank enemy surface craft, and pummeled enemy land fortifications and troops.

The following four drawings show some ships in action.

Figure IX-1. PC 550 on patrol off Anzio, Italy, 15 September 1943. Note the British cruiser at the right and the early type radar on the mast of the PC. This drawing is by and courtesy of Robert Baldwin.

Figure IX-2. In this drawing the artist depicts PC 543, off Gela, Sicily on 10 July 1943, destroying a German bomber while escorting the submarine HMS *Safari*. In the background DD USS *Maddox* explodes from a bomb that penetrated her depth charge magazine. This drawing is by and courtesy of Robert Baldwin.

Figure IX-3. This picture shows PC 543 laying a depth charge pattern on a submarine contact in the Mediterranean. Note two depth charges in the air fired from the K-guns. This painting was by and is courtesy of Robert Baldwin.

Figure IX-4. PC 543 in the van of the first wave of landing craft at Anzio, Italy, 22 January 1944. In the background a British LCT showers the beach with rockets. This drawing is by and courtesy of Robert Baldwin.

Damage, destruction, and death struck in many places and to many vessels on the sea, and small ships suffered their casualties along with the larger ships. Some small ships also succumbed to the violent winds and pounding seas of hurricanes, williwaws, and typhoons.

After sinking the German submarine U-375, the PC 624 became a casualty dragging anchor and running against rocks during a storm. A black and white rendition of the painting of the ship is on the next page.

Figure IX-5. PC 624, shown in this painting, dragged anchor and ran aground during a storm off Palermo, Sicily on 12 August 1943. The painting was by and is courtesy of Robert Baldwin.

One of the most important, dramatic, costly, and remembered actions of World War II was the invasion of France at Normandy on 6 June 1944 by Allied Forces. Thousands of ships, large and small, brought troops, firepower, and materiel to the beachheads. It was the largest amphibious operation in history, and its success depended heavily on the actions of hundreds of United States Navy and Coast Guard small craft.

They swept mines and other obstacles. They led landing craft to the beaches. They pounded German positions with their guns. They transported men and supplies across the channel and to and from the beaches. And they saved the lives of many soldiers and sailors by pulling exhausted, wounded men from the sea. Some of these actions are recorded in the next drawing of the D-Day landing.

Figure IX-6. This rendition of the landing at Normandy on D-Day shows various landing craft and small ships in action. The drawing is from the USCG Patrol – For the Tars and Spars of the Boston District. a monthly publication of the U. S. Coast Guard, Boston District, Volume 2, No. 7, June 1944. It is courtesy of Donald F. Townsend.

Other small craft were lost to shells that exploded against their hulls, aerial bombs that bore through their decks and exploded in inner compartments, mines that erupted on contact that tore their hulls apart, and torpedoes that streaked through the water and blasted them open. Wounded and dead men lay on their decks and in compartments below decks or went missing.

When a small ship took a serious hit, the captain and crew had only minutes, or even maybe only seconds, in which to decide if the ship could continue fighting or if the blow was fatal. When the most feared order of all, "Abandon Ship," rang out about the decks and spaces below, men soon found themselves drifting among high waves struggling for life and staring across the waves as the ocean swallowed their ship. One sailor recalled this painful and frightening experience with a painting.

Figure IX-7. This is a black and white rendition of a painting by Carter Barber who watched his ship, PC 496, slip beneath the waves. A color copy is in the Section titled Color Plates. It is courtesy of Carter Barber.

Danger was ever present at sea on the smaller vessels. Waves burst aboard and stormed over the decks. Heavy seas bent and twisted steel beams and bulkheads. Seas tore at and ripped out stanchions, ammunition lockers, life rafts, and even 3"-50 guns bolted to the deck. Waves grasped and heaved sailors overboard. Men were lost at sea, their memorial service the sadness of their shipmates, their burial site the vast endless ocean. One sailor recorded such an episode in verse.

SEPTEMBER 30, 1943

It's up in the morning before daylight,
The sea is rough, nothing in sight.
The Captain gives an order for a change of course,
So we ride with the wind and the rain's full force.

The barometer is falling and the rains increase,
The waves get higher, the winds never cease.
The sea moans and tears at the ship,
Everything is lashed down so it will not slip.

One life raft is ripped from the port rail,
The bow is under, then next the fantail.
Then the ship lurches with a sickening roll,
Two men are washed over, the sea wants its toll.

One man bobs up and comes in sight,
The other is lost in the sea's terrible might,
We are backing down into the storm,
Trying our best to save this human form.

The wind gets stronger, the waves seem to mock,
The ship groans and bucks like a bronc,
Lookouts are pointing at the floating man,
Who is shouting, kicking, and waving his hands.

It is nearly an hour before he is alongside,
We bring him aboard, we have saved his hide.
Every man is silent, no smile on his face,
One man was lost without a trace.

We've fought a battle to win if we can,
But the sea has won, it has claimed a man.

Melvin L. DeWitt composed this poem on 30 September 1943.

In addition to taking their own casualties and loss of men at sea, men on small ships frequently rushed to the rescue of many other shipmates, merchant men, soldiers, and even enemy servicemen. When they did, they gave their utmost to help others. They rescued some, but watched helplessly as ships' hulls crushed other men between them, freezing water turned men into lifeless rigid forms, or the sea pulled them down before they could be saved.

One particular episode stands out in the minds and memories and hearts of many small ship sailors who raced to the scene to help save survivors of a troop ship loaded with soldiers. It was the sinking of troop ship SS *Leopoldville* on 24 December 1944. The following poem captures some of the essence of that tragedy.

A CHANNEL NIGHTMARE

By winter, 1944, the war had spanned five years;
The horrors of invasion had muffled any cheers.
A German breakthrough at the Bulge,
an SOS went out.
The 66th Was ready; the order said, "Move out!"

There were turkeys in the mess hall
as we went to the shore,
But Christmas dinner's not important
when the battle starts to roar.

I'm sure the thought was in our minds;
"This is the Christmas season!"
Why couldn't we have had a truce,
that surely is a reason.

We started off across the foam
and headed out for France,
But the way the Fates decreed it,
we never had a chance.

The U-boat took its final mark;
the "fish" began its run.
In a matter of just seconds
its deadly work was done!

A blast was unexpected;
confusion ruled the day.
The crew took off in lifeboats
and that left Hell to pay.

Heroics were quite commonplace
for that wonderful G. I.,
But hundreds now had perished,
and I'm sure some wondered why.

Yet, now, the rescuers appeared,
some were British, some were Yanks.
They dragged exhausted men aboard
whose bruised lips murmured, "Thanks."

And as these saviors bobbed around
within a floodlight's beam
The hellish scene they witnessed
was surely a bad dream.

For corpses floated everywhere
upon the Channel tossed.
When the final list was published,
800 men were lost.

Survivors once again use "Thanks!,"
be it a verb or noun
For they'll remember always
when the *Leopoldville* went down!!

This poem is presented here courtesy of Wesley G. Johnson.

Except for the times when called to General Quarters after a Ping Jockey heard what seemed like a metallic response from a sound pulse, convoy duty was monotonous and boring.

Men stood watches four hours on and eight hours off, ate meals and slept when the sea conditions permitted, and they read and wrote letters. Some of them also used their skills at hand crafts to make jewelry and other items from ship's materials or expended ammunition casings. One such item, a pencil holder, is shown.

Figure IX-8. This pencil holder made from a 40mm shell was embellished with a Navy emblem. The lieutenant made this pencil holder "while doing boring convoy escort duty between New York, Guantanamo and Trinidad." The photograph is courtesy of Herbert Katzenberg.

The military campaign in the Pacific Ocean was noted for its island hopping – invasions of one island after another in the advance toward the islands of Japan. It seemed that ships and men barely settled into one place when they were off for another place. They were always jumping off to another place. This idea was summarized in this short ditty.

THE SOUTH WEST PACIFIC
Some call it the South West Pacific
Land of the slow easy race.
Some even say it's terrific.
Me!!!! I call it the "Jumping Off Place."

Ed Sidebottom composed this ditty. It is courtesy of Ed Sidebottom.

Many of the small ships, along with the larger vessels, suffered through air attacks. During escort or picket duty and while herding landing craft to invasion beaches the enemy planes pounded them with bombs and machine gun fire. The small ships fought back and some of them took casualties. Crew members suffered wounds and died, and bombs and shells tore holes in ships and sank some.

Gunners on quite a few of the small ships manned their weapons and pounded 20mm, 40mm, and 3 inch shells into German, Italian, and Japanese aircraft. They drove off and damaged the enemy planes and knocked many of them from the sky, watching them trail smoke and crash into the water.

On some occasions the enemy threw new weapons against them. One such weapon was a variant of the rocket powered V1 and V2 missiles and others used against England. This weapon was the Glide Bomb that the Germans dropped from an aircraft. One man's impression of a glide bomb that attacked and almost sank his ship is on the next page.

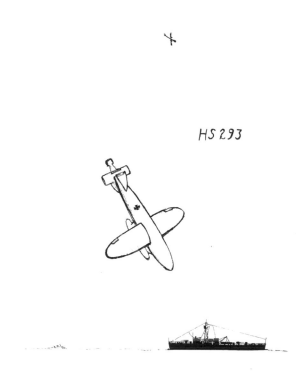

Figure IX-9. Douglas L. Roberts drew this impression of an attack by an HS293 German glide bomb on SC 648. It is courtesy of Douglas Roberts.

Also, the ships lobbed shells into islands before and during invasions. When they did these feats the men on the ships proudly displayed their results by painting swastikas, rising suns, or replicas of islands on the superstructures of their ships.

Three examples of this "victory art" for downed aircraft and bombardments are shown on two following pages.

South Pacific – circa 1945. on left: Lt. Allison M. Levy, Engineering
Officer; center, name unknown; and Joe Graig (nee Gonzales), SK 3C.

Figure IX-10. Here Allison M. Levy and Joe Craig, on PC 623 in 1945 hold a flag painted to show two Japanese planes shot down and five islands bombarded. It is courtesy of the Patrol Craft Sailors Association Newsletter, Issue Number 34, Oct,-Dec., 1996.

Flying bridge of USS PCE(R)-849, soldiers and sailors working together. (Courtesy of John J. Reinhart.)

Figure IX-11. Crew members and some soldiers on PCER 849 point to their handiwork depicting four Japanese planes downed and five islands struck. The photograph is courtesy of the Patrol Craft Sailors Association.

Figure IX-12. This photograph of the bridge of SC 743 shows artistic evidence of four Japanese planes downed at Arawc harbor "in a brief but bloody skirmish." The photograph is courtesy of Theodore Treadwell.

Many other ships attacked sound contacts with depth charges and mousetraps, but without conclusive positive results. Later discoveries or data confirmed that some attacks were successful, such as that of PC 566. On 30 July 1942, the PC 566 attacked a sound contact off the coast of Louisiana while escorting the freighter *Robert E. Lee.* The result was not definite. Fifty-nine years later explorers discovered the sunken U-166. The Navy concluded that PC 566 had sunk the U-Boat.

Despite the lack of evidence of damage to a submarine, many of these attacks had positive consequences. Frequently the attacks damaged submarines, drove them away from their intended targets, or prevented submarine captains from firing their torpedoes. Either of these events resulted in the possibility of saving a target vessel such as a merchant ship in a convoy.

In some instances the Navy awarded a "probable" sinking of a submarine. In other cases official notice was not awarded, but the officers and crews of the ships involved felt certain they had scored damage or a kill. When a kill was an unofficial probable the crew sometimes put a symbol on display inside the ship such as the one shown here.

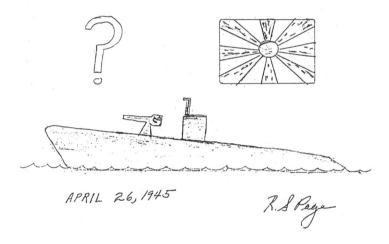

APRIL 26, 1945   R. S Page

Figure IX-13. This sketch, drawn by Raymond Page, represents the probable sinking of a Japanese submarine at Adak Island in the Aleutians. It was posted in the chartroom of PC 793. It is from the author's collection.

In some cases of the many attacks by small ships on submarines ample evidence of underwater explosions and debris from the submarine that floated to the surface confirmed the sinking of a submarine. In such instances the United States Navy acknowledged the attacking ships with a "sure kill." In these cases crew members decorated their ships with a symbol of a submarine and possibly a swastika or rising sun as appropriate. Two such elements of this kind of war art are given here.

Figure IX-14. This photograph shows George Raab admiring the symbols for his ship, PC 619, sinking a U-Boat and downing a German bomber. The photograph is courtesy of Ray Goin.

Figure IX-15. Here an artist on PC 487 records the ship's confirmed kill of a Japanese submarine. This is a U. S. Navy photograph.

The escort ships, subchasers, minesweepers, and Coast Guard Cutters of the United States Navy in World War II served in all theaters of war. Around the globe they performed the traditional missions for which they were designed and also many others when the need arose. Some of them labored in convoys along the coasts of the Americas protecting merchant ships from U-Boats. Others patrolled the Pacific coasts of the United States warding off Japanese intruders. Numerous of them beat against savage seas escorting troops and supplies to forward bases for the assaults on Germany and Japan.

All of them contributed to winning the war whether their duty was near the "States," or on far away seas, or off distant islands and foreign lands. Like other fighting ships, the small ships counted their victories and also suffered their casualties. Ships were damaged, destroyed, and sunk. Their sailors bled and died. Through it all the men kept their spirits and, as illustrated in this Chapter, produced art, humor, and artifacts that helped record their efforts and sacrifices.

CHAPTER X

OTHER CONTRIBUTORS

During and after World War II numerous persons who did not serve on small ships had then and still have interest in them and the men who sailed them. These persons composed poems about naval service, drew and painted cartoons and pictures of sailors and ships, constructed models of small ships, and even remodeled or restored a few of them. Some of their work was published and publically displayed or used, but much of it remains in personal files and family archives or is on limited display. This chapter contains some of the many items produced by other than small ship sailors that has not been generally available but that has relevance to the ships and their crews.

After World War II companies and even individuals purchased decommissioned ships from the Navy. The buyers converted some of them for commercial use and others for personal use as yachts. One ship that still serves today in commercial use and retains many of its original features is used as a cruise boat in Florida.[22] Before this final use, it changed hands many times for may different uses. A picture of it is given here, and a photograph of it in its World War II configuration is shown in Appendix B.

Figure X-1. This is a recent photograph of *Black Tie* (ex YP 611). It is one of the few World War II small ships still in active civilian service. The photograph is courtesy of Conrad Brown.

Many persons have drawn and published sketches and plans of the capital ships that participated in World War II. Numerous books and nautical and military journals also contain many such plans. These plans are of interest to naval architects and engineers, historians, and ship model builders.

Few books and journals, however, produced line drawings and plans of some of the small ships that are considered in this book. They are of interest to a similar community of technical persons, historians, and ship model builders. Many ship modelers have shown enthusiasm for the plans because the plans have not been widely known or distributed. Some of the sources of small ship drawings and plans that are known to the author are given in this Chapter and in the Bibliography.

Two unique sets of ship's plans are of interest. They are both of a PC. The first plan, not in a book or journal, was drawn by John B. Tombaugh, an historian and draftsman.

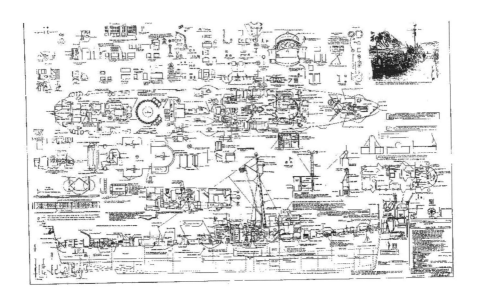

Figure X-2. This figure is a reduced version of a plan for the PC 461 class. It may not be useable as a working plan, but it shows the detail and care with which the plan was drawn. A larger version of the figure is in the book *PC Patrol Craft of World War II* by the author and listed in the Bibliography.

Blueprint size drawings also are available from John Tombaugh who drew the plans.[23]

The second set of unique plans shown starting on the next page is from a Polish source. The plans are shown in three figures.

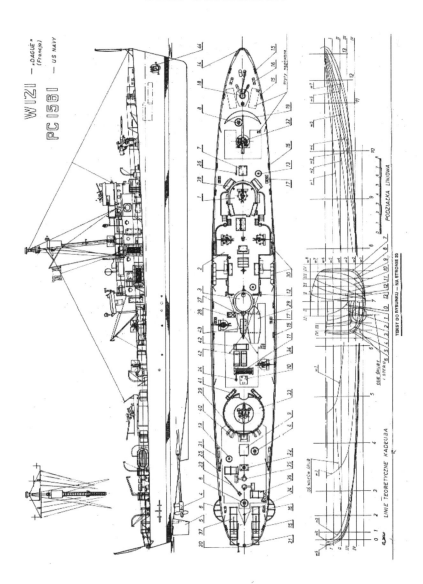

Figure X-3. This sketch of plans for ex PC 1561 that became W121, *Dague*, of France is from Patrolowiec, Pozialka 1:80, Data 1988 r. It is courtesy of Andrej Mista.

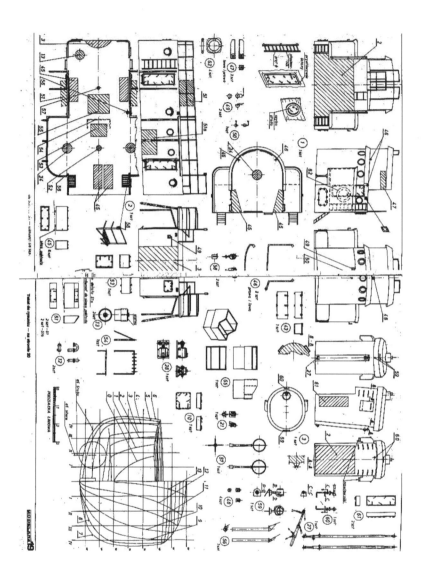

Figure X-4. This sketch of some details of the plans for ex PC 1561 that became W121, *Dague*, of France is from Patrolowiec, Pozialka 1:80, Data 1988 r. It is courtesy of Andrej Mista.

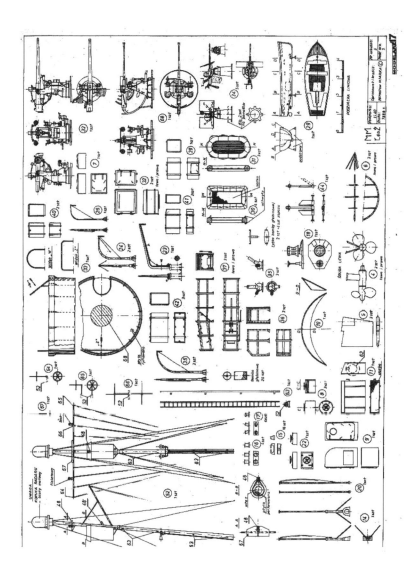

Figure X-5. This sketch of some details of the plans for ex PC 1561 that became W121, *Dague*, of France is from Patrolowiec, Pozialka 1:80, Data 1988 r. It is courtesy of Andrej Mista.

Two other plans by John Tombaugh for a YMS and an AM are given in the next two figures.

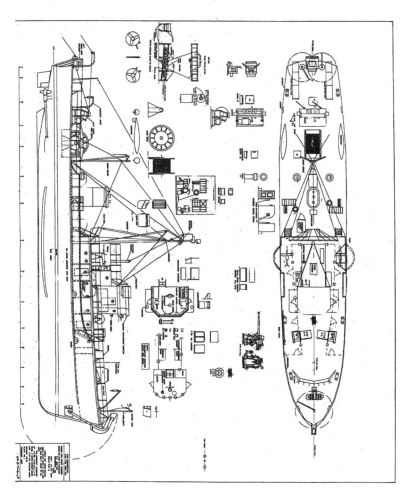

Figure X-6. This scale 1:48 TH plan for YMS 135-445, MSC minesweeper was drawn by and is courtesy of John B. Tombaugh.

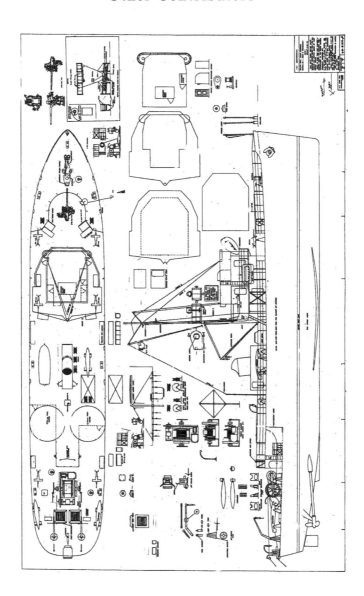

Figure X-7. This scale 1:48 TH plan for AM.1 minesweeper was drawn by and is courtesy of John B. Tombaugh.

Ship modelers used these plans and other plans from private and government sources to design and construct models of various small ships. Some of the plans and models remain in the builders' personal collections. Other ship modelers donated their models to museums and other organizations that present naval displays to the public.

Other persons around the United States and in other countries also made models of some small ships. One of particular interest is a model of a PC, such as those that were transferred to France during and after World War II.[24] The model operates on batteries. A photograph of the model that looks like a PC breasting a moderate sea is from a public demonstration in France.

Figure X-8. French model of a PC of the 461 class. It was numbered PC 32 by the builder. Michel Lelievre made the model in 1996 from a 1/100 eme plan of the Musee de la Marine: Escorteur cotier Lansquenet. He powered it with 12 volt batteries, and made it radio controlled. The photograph is courtesy of Michel Lelievre.

Figure X-9. Shown above is a photograph of another model of a PC made by Lelievre and numbered W 26. Behind the PC model is a model of a tug boat also made by Lelievre. He displayed these models at the French Navy Base of Brest (Marine Nationale, Arsenal de Brest). The photograph is courtesy of Michel Lelievre. A color copy is in the Section titled Color Plates to show the typical colors of a PC and most other small ships.

Another favorite World War II ship among model ship builders is the 110 foot, wooden SC subchaser. A black and white version of a painting of a cutaway view of SC 497 is shown on the next page. This drawing was commissioned by Theodore R. Treadwell, commanding officer of the ship during World War II. It displays many of the details ship modelers need to build an SC model. At the request of Ted Treadwell, David P. Lawrence drew this cutaway view in black and white in 1997. Colors were added digitally. The drawing is © Ted Treadwell who used it in his book *Splinter Fleet,* listed in the Bibliography. A color copy is in the Section titled Color Plates.

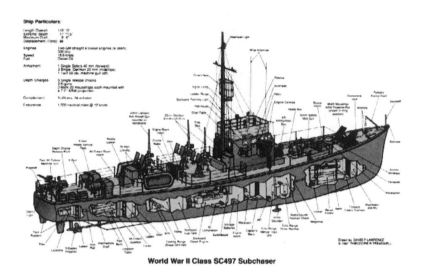

World War II Class SC497 Subchaser

Figure X-10. This cutaway view of SC 497 is courtesy of Ted Treadwell. A larger size in color is in the Section titled Color Plates.

One model of an SC built by a friend of a former Captain of an SC is on the next page. Stephen Greeley Clarke, a World War II United States Army paratrooper in Europe and later a Professor of Chemistry, built the model. He started from scratch with a block of white pine that he air dried and heat treated for a year before he began carving the hull. He scaled the model to specifications he got from plans supplied by the U. S. Navy BUSHIPS and from the Sparkman and Stevens Naval Architects.

Figure X-11. This model of SC 677 was made in 1977 by Stephen Greeley Clarke for Page G. Harman, C. O. of SC 677 in the Pacific. The photograph is courtesy of Page G. Harman.

Figure X-12. This unusual construction is a card model (paper) of SC 1029 to 1:250 scale. Darius Lipinski designed it in 2001, and it was made by and is available from Paper-Lab Publishing of Canada. The photograph is courtesy of Darius Lipinski.

In addition to models, some persons and organizations obtained small ships and rebuilt and decorated them. For example, the Greenpeace organization purchased ex PC 1120 after World War II, remodeled it, and embellished the bow of the ship with a whale and dolphin insignia.[25] A photograph of the ship named *Ohana Kai* is shown in the following figure.

Figure X-13. Photograph of *Ohana Kai* (ex PC 1120) under Greenpeace ownership, about 1977. Note the raised bow, white paint, and whale and dolphin insignia on the starboard bow. The photograph is courtesy of Nora McCarthy of Greenpeace.

Persons who were not in the Navy or Coast Guard understood and appreciated the mystique of sailors that attracted the ladies to them. Ladies fell for not only the confident swagger of sailors but also their tailor made, tight fitting, jumpers and bell bottom trousers and their jaunty white hats tucked back with a burst of wavy hair jutting from in front. Sailors were different from soldiers in ways that many persons recognized and took pleasure in watching. I present here a pair of cartoons emphasizing the difference between soldiers and sailors and their interests when on liberty.

A SAILOR IN MAIN-ST.

Figure X-14. This cartoon was from a serviceman's newspaper on Gibralter. It was named <u>THE ROCK – The Link With Home</u>, Anniversary Number, Vol. 3, No. 1, March 1943. It is courtesy of George Amaral.

AN AIRMAN OFF MAIN-ST.
"Would you care to see the Gibraltar Museum, señorita?"

Figure X-15. This cartoon was from <u>THE ROCK – The Link With Home</u>, Anniversary Number, Vol. 3, No. 1, March 1943. It is courtesy of George Amaral.

People also knew what all servicemen, especially sailors after long times at sea, wanted. Along with mail from home sailors wanted liberty in some exotic port and a chance to meet some special girl, maybe like the one posing on the next page.

Figure X-16. This cartoon was from a serviceman's newspaper by and for men serving on Gibralter. <u>THE ROCK – The Link With Home</u>, Anniversary Number, Vol. 3, No. 1, March 1943. It is courtesy of George Amaral.

Sailors of the Navy of the United States were known for their desire for fun-filled liberties when ashore. Besides their interest in the ladies, they were not averse to having a few drinks to help relax and forget their days at sea. Some people thought them to consume alcohol a bit excessively and to be "sinful and ginful." The following poem helps justify their opinions.

THREE SCORE AND TEN

The horse and mule live thirty years,
And nothing know of wines and beers;
The goat and sheep at twenty die,
And never taste of scotch and rye;
The cow drinks water by the ton,
And at eighteen is mostly done;
The dog at fifteen cashes in,
Without the aid of rum and gin;
The cat in milk and water soaks,
And then in twelve short years it croaks;
The modest sober, bone-dry hen,
Lays eggs for nogs and dies at ten;
All animals are strictly dry,
They sinless live and swiftly die;
But sinful, ginful, NAVY men,
Survive for three score years and ten!

The person who wrote this poem is unknown. It was submitted by Bob Crowl, PC566 to the PCSA News and appeared on Page 5, Issue Number 8.

Among the many invasions in which numerous small ships participated was the invasion of Iwo Jima. Thanks to one special photograph of Marines raising the flag of the United States of America during that nightmare, the world will always recall the struggle and terrible loss of life on that island.

The following poem recalls the battle of Iwo Jima and illustrates how proud and grateful people were for what members of the Navy, Coast Guard, and Marine Corps did at that place.

D DAY IWO JIMA, FEBRUARY 19, 1945

I was on a heavy cruiser,
In the old Pacific Isles,
Off the shores of Iwo Jima,
We fought for quite a while.

I thought about my sweetheart,
My mother and my Dad,
All about Old America,
And the good times I had.

We would tune in on the radio,
To get punched in the nose,
With a message of sympathy,
From Tokyo Rose.

She told us we were losing,
That America could not win,
That our wives and our sweethearts,
Were going with other men.

It was early in the morning,
On the dot at nine o'clock,
We opened up the fireworks,
And the old ship began to rock.

We bombarded the island,
From the middle to the end,
But as you know without a doubt,
We lost a lot of men.

They gave us reinforcements,
To replace the dead,
And early in the afternoon,
The marines pushed ahead.

The Japanese were tough and rugged,
They thought they could stand,
But we as young Americans,
Showed them we could land.

We had to take old Iwo,
To protect our land,
The Japanese were refueling there,
And bombing old Saipan.

We finally secured the air field,
And stopped the heavy blow,
And then we sent our B-29's,
Right into Tokyo.

There was a boy from a Western state,
I'm sure that you know his name,
He helped raise the flag on Iwo,
To keep America's fame.

Now the war is over,
The envy and the strife,
But in my heart a memory,
For those who lost their life.

This poem was composed by W. J. Rawlins who served on USS *Chester*, CA 27. It is courtesy of Gary W. Johnson, grandson of W. J. Rawlins.

During and since World War II many persons expressed and still show interest in and empathy for the small ships and their rugged sailors. They displayed their feelings through art, cartoons, ship models, and other crafts. Of those persons a small group is represented here through the works of art, handcrafts, and writing that showed their concern for the small ship sailors.

CHAPTER XI

GOING HOME

After the Allied victory in Europe the campaign against Japan in the Pacific intensified. Military bases around the Pacific grew in size with materiel and men needed to launch the invasion of the Japanese homeland. That final stage in the island hopping campaign would be the largest and the most costly of all battles so far. On 6 August 1945 and 9 August 1945, however, the blasts that vaporized Hiroshima and Nagasaki signaled that the end of the war was near.

Hundreds of thousands, possibly even millions, of lives would be spared the devastation of the ferocious battles that planners expected in the effort to gain foothold on and conquer the Japanese islands. Whatever else may be argued, the two atomic explosions over Japan were a blessing to the men and women of all countries who would have been involved in the prolonged slaughter that the Japanese fanatical and suicidal defenders had planned.

Men of the United States Navy and Coast Guard, who had spent months and years among the Pacific islands especially rejoiced after the long years of fighting in the Pacific. Their commanders also were relieved because they did not have the burden of sending men off to further battles. One man wrote a poem that summed up life and war on a YMS and that they were finally going home.

THE MIGHTY YMS

Designed to be a mere district craft
all one hundred thirty six feet, fore and aft;
we sail the seas so very far
thousands of miles from the nearest bar.
We are the boys of the YARD MINE SWEEPER,
who sail the seas with God as our keeper.

We sail under the call of Gracious Nine,
a finer bunch of men (?) you could never find.
With feet of lead and backs of steel
they stand and sweat behind the wheel.
Oh, we're the boys of the YARD MINE SWEEPER,
who sail the seas with God as our keeper.

In port we eat steak and turkey so good,
at sea we eat what no human would,
We sail not through the sea but over and under.
We rise high on one crest and then down we thunder.
Oh, we're the boys of the YARD MINE SWEEPER,
who sail the seas with God as our keeper.

First in Wakayama, Otake, and Kure Ko,
it seems we were always on the go.
Altho no mines we ever got
we were always there upon the spot.

Oh, we're the boys of the YARD MINE SWEEPER,
who sail the seas with God as our keeper.
Now for home we're bound at last,
soon to forget the horrible past;
if the GM's will keep pounding away
and the solder in number one will only stay
Oh, we're the boys of the YARD MINE SWEEPER,
who sail the seas with God as our keeper.

William Skafke wrote this poem on YMS 289. It is courtesy of Jack M. Passmann.

When World War II ended, naval commands around the world issued thanks for the end of the war. One such item was a telegram from Vice Admiral Frank Jack Fletcher.

Despfit Form No. 95   U. S. S. ....PC 793..........   N. O. B. Navy 230 6-29-45 10M.

(090 V NUD) -P-F-A- NUD 142325 ADFU CRAG ALAG ALAW APER APOG APOP GR 161

STATEMENT OF VICE ADMIRAL FRANK JACK FLETCHER U.S. NAVY ON OFFICIAL ANNOUNCEMENT BY THE PRESIDENT OF VICTORY OVER JAPAN "WELL DONE" TO ALL THE OFFICERS AND MEN OF THE NORTHPACIFIC FORCE AND ALASKAN SEA FRONTIER. I ASSURE THEIR FAMILIES AT HOME THAT THEIR PART IN BRINGING JAPAN TO HER KNEES HAS BEEN AN IMPORTANT ONE. OURS HAS NOT BEEN A SPECTACULAR JOB, BUT ALL THOSE WHO HELPED DRIVE THE INVADER FROM THE ALEUTIANS, HAMMERED FROM SEA AND AIR AT HIS KOREALS OUTPOSTS, OR WORKED IN THE WILLIAWAS TO PREPARE FOR FUTURE BLOWS -NOW HAPPILY NOT NEEDED- CAN WELL BE PROUD PARTICIPANTS IN TODAY'S VICTORY. LET US CELEBRATE THIS DAY NOT IN TRIUMPH, BUT WITH THANKSGIVING AND GRATITUDE. LET US NOT FORGET OUR COMRADES WHO CANNOT SHARE IT. THE WORLD IS NOW AT PEACE. LET US FACE THE PROBLEMS THAT WILL CONFRONT US WITH THE SAME SPIRIT WHICH HAS WON THIS TERRIBLE WAR.

| Ø342:TOR | OPR:ML | 255Ø KCS | 14 AUGUST 1945 |
| SYSTEM | | PRECEDENCE | CLASSIFICATION |

FROM: RADIO ADAK, ALASKA

ACTION TO: ALL SHIPS AND SECTORS NORTH PACIFIC.

Figure XI-1. This telegram expressed Vice Admiral Fletcher's thanks to his command. It is from the author's collection.

Immediately after World War II the United States Navy was eager to dispose of its large fleet of ships and to release from active duty the many reservists who had served the Navy and the Coast Guard so well during the war. The great majority of the men in blues were just as eager to leave their ships, shed those blues, and go home.

Getting released from the armed services did not happen immediately, though, and it became a tedious and agonizing process for each man of counting "points" that he needed to be discharged. The government awarded those points to service men for their age, their number of months in service, family responsibilities, and other factors. When one amassed a sufficient number of points, according to a schedule that varied with time after the end of hostilities, one got the notice to be separated from a ship or station and to head for a Separation Center to be processed and discharged.

The procedure was not that clear cut, however, because many men had enough points for discharge but could not be released because they were essential to operate their ships. The Navy kept them aboard ship months beyond their time for discharge according to the point schedule. Despite their disappointment at watching shipmates heave their Sea Bags over their shoulders and stride down the gangway of their ships on their way home, while they remained aboard, the men who remained stayed and did their duty.

Remaining on board ship provided them time to ponder where they had been, what they had done, shipmates they had known and lost, and friendships they would remember. They had time to reflect on their tough sea-going ordeal and to speculate on who among them would be the last to go, to leave the ship. This experience of waiting and wondering is summed up in the following poem.

THE LEGEND OF THE PC

Listen my children, and I shall tell,
Of three long years I spent in hell
On earth aboard a mighty ship
I remember it all quite well.

It was on June 3rd in '42
And scarce a man yet in the crew
Remembers that famous day and year,
And swarmed aboard without any fear,
We boys in Navy blues.

To the greater part it was quite new,
Except to a chosen, salty few,
But far from sniveling cowards, we
Boldly sailed to open sea,
This rough and rugged crew.

Who soon became a seasoned gang,
Who didn't give the slightest hang,
Whether 'twas rough, or whether 'twas fair,
Regardless of weather, we were right there,
When down the curtain rang.

Down through the Caribbean blue,
Sailed this wild and wooly crew,
With an eye for adventure, and come what may,
We had our time to laugh and to play,
When our work was through.

Over many a thundering mountainous swell
Our stalwart bow both rose. and fell,
With a jarring crash that shook all beams,
Until we thought that all the seams,
Would burst, and leave an empty shell.

After two years of this rugged duty
And teasing with some Spanish cutie;
A few short days we had at home,
Then set sail across the foam
To view some different foreign beauty.

On Christmas day of '44
We lay just off a foreign shore.
When from a clear sky, there came that day,
An order – and we were under way
Toward that life we love, once more.

Then the talk flew night and day,
Of who would go and who would stay,
Who were the lucky ones to leave,
Who were the sorry ones to grieve,
The parting of the way.

Through the years of traveling on,
Many have come, and many have gone,
Until there's left but a faithful few
Of the old rugged, and salty crew,
To greet each breaking dawn.

But now there comes, as always will,
That one last bitter choking pill.
Of who goes on his merry way,
And who regretfully has to stay
And carry on the struggle still.

This poem was written by R. H. Rushing who served on PC 466.

Most small ship sailors, like sailors on larger ships, wanted nothing more than to return home and pin onto their civvies the "Ruptured Duck" emblem that showed that they were veterans of World War II.

In Circular No. 454 dated 29 Nov 1944, the War Department adopted an honorable discharge emblem for wear on the uniforms of all military personnel who were discharged or separated from the service under honorable conditions. The emblem was a navy blue, diamond-shaped, cloth insignia depicting a gold colored eagle surrounded by a gold wreath.

Men wore the insignia on the right breast of their uniforms with the long axis of the lozenge horizontal. The United States Navy issued the insignia to naval service personnel who were about to leave or had left the military service with an Honorable Discharge. The government also allowed the veterans to wear their uniforms for up to thirty days after they were discharged to give them time to find civilian clothes and because there was a clothing shortage.

The emblem was to be worn as a badge of honor indicative of honest and faithful service while a member of the Armed Forces. Though the eagle symbol was not created by a small ship sailor I reproduce it here as a contribution of the

United States to all servicemen including the small ship sailors.

To many servicemen the eagle in the discharge emblem looked like a duck, and, because the men were eager to go home, they wanted to "Take off like a Ruptured Duck." That saying, that was popular among servicemen during the war, probably influenced how the ex-service members gave that nickname "Ruptured Duck" to the discharge emblem.

Figure XI-2. This figure is a black and white replica of the famous "Ruptured Duck" emblem honorably discharged members of the United States Navy wore on their uniforms after World War II. The emblem is shown in color in the Section titled Color Plates. It is from the author's collection.

After discharge and doffing their uniforms, men and women who had served in the armed forces were allowed to wear a similar symbol as a lapel pin on their civilian jackets or as a pin on other types of civilian clothing. Variations of this pin also are shown.

Figures XI-3 and XI- 4. Two other versions of the discharge pin for civilian wear. It is from the author's collection.

After their return to civilian life, all members of the armed services received a letter from President Truman. In it he expressed the nation's gratitude for what the service men and women had done.

WILLIAM JOHN VEIGELE Jr.

To you who answered the call of your country and served in its Armed Forces to bring about the total defeat of the enemy, I extend the heartfelt thanks of a grateful Nation. As one of the Nation's finest, you undertook the most severe task one can be called upon to perform. Because you demonstrated the fortitude, resourcefulness and calm judgment necessary to carry out that task, we now look to you for leadership and example in further exalting our country in peace.

Harry Truman

THE WHITE HOUSE

Figure XI-5. President Harry S. Truman sent this letter to all discharged members of the armed forces. Note that he addressed it to each individual by name. It is from the author's collection.

For the fiftieth anniversary of the participation of the United States in World War II the government designed another symbol made in different forms. It also used the eagle or "Ruptured Duck" symbol.

Figure XI-6. This image of a colored patch to be worn on hats or jackets commemorates the participation of the United States in World War II. It uses the eagle or "Ruptured Duck" as did the discharge emblems. A color copy is in the Section titled Color Plates. It is courtesy of Alex Kilpatrick.

For men of the small ship navy the duck symbol was even more significant than it was to other servicemen and women. It seemed prophetic to small ship sailors that the symbol they would wear to prove that they had served during World War II on one of the special type of ships that were part of the "Donald Duck Navy" was a "Ruptured Duck."

Soon after the war ended the United States Navy rushed to dismantle its huge fleet. Battleships, carriers, cruisers, destroyers, submarines, and the small ships of all types began to disappear. Some sank as target ships. Others felt the sting of the atom bombs at Bikini. Many exchanged their ensigns for those of foreign nations. Scrappers tore out the bowels and flensed the hulls off many ships, turning them into scrap. A few ships served the United States for decades in lesser roles before being destroyed. Some rusted and decayed into almost unrecognizable hulks in junk yards. Only a handful survive as converted work boats or private yachts.

The only one that has been preserved as an historical memorial is USS *Hazard* AM 240 (built on a PCE hull) that rests landlocked in Freedom Park, Omaha, Nebraska. A photograph of *Hazard* is shown in Appendix B.

It is a sad end to these sturdy ships and their gallant crews, and it brings to mind the first stanza of a poem about Old Ironsides by Oliver Wendell Holmes.

AY, TEAR HER TATTERED ENSIGN DOWN!

Ay, tear her tattered ensign down!
Long has it waved on high,
And many an eye has danced to see
That banner in the sky;
Beneath it rung the battle shout,
And burst the cannon's roar; –
The meteor of the ocean air
Shall sweep the clouds no more.

CHAPTER XII

THE LATER YEARS

A small number of the many small ship sailors who enlisted or received commissions in the United States Navy and Coast Guard Reserves "shipped over"at the end of the war and stayed in the Regular Navy or Coast Guard. Some other men never returned home. They were buried at sea or in graves far from home. Those who did return home safely felt and expressed gratitude that they had survived the war. They remained mindful, though, of their lost shipmates, and they respected their sacrifices and memories. Despite their sad memories, however, they knew, more than before, that their lives were precious and they had to proceed with their lives. With a strong feeling of respect for the shipmates they lost, the men who left the service showed delight in their own return to civilian life.

After a few years in the United States armed services during World War II, with their regimentation, uniforms, obedience to authority, responsibilities, thrills, and dangers, those who went home found civilian life challenging. Civilian clothing left years before in closets at home no longer fit or matched the new styles. Freedom to go where and when they wanted to made choosing what to do difficult at first. They found it easy to talk to ex-servicemen but hesitant with and some times intolerant of the "problems" civilians complained about. Civilian life was different from military life, but the returned sailors adjusted quickly as they had adjusted a few years earlier to naval life.

For many years after their release from the Navy, most men were happy to be away from the war and Navy life. They busied themselves catching up on the years of civilian life they had missed while they were being tossed about the oceans, fighting boredom, chasing and dodging the enemy, and living with danger. Fun, sports, jobs, careers, education, marriage, and families now consumed their interests. Most men gave less and less thought to their sea service experience because they now were engaged in new, exciting, civilian adventures.

But the concluding words in the poem titled **"Ain't it the Truth"** by Tony Rego were prophetic. He wrote,

"And in later years we may laugh at all this,
And there may be a time when we'll find that we'll miss
Some of this life, that we know so well,
And may wish we were back a board – who can tell."

As years passed and the young men who fought the war became middle aged men, many of them reminisced about their service days and the life "we know so well." They longed for the camaraderie of their former shipmates. And they, in their minds' eyes at least, would "wish we were back aboard."

Nostalgia for their seagoing days urged them to contact former shipmates. In some cases age imposed a barrier that many men found it hard to accept as shown in the next cartoon.

Figure XII-1. This cartoon by Lee Barber shows the impact of years on the former young men who sailed patrol craft during World War II. It is courtesy of Lee Barber of PCS 1389.

When men found shipmates they held ships' reunions. These events were so emotional and rewarding for most men that they decided to expand the gatherings by banding together with other ships' reunions.

This effort, that was a particularly creative organizational endeavor, by Patrick Ward (Yeoman 2/C, PC 565) and Wesley G. Johnson (Lt., PC 564), led to the founding in 1986 of the Patrol Craft Sailors Society. They assigned it the motto "We Were Too Good To Be Forgotten." The society began issuing a newsletter to participants. They named it the "Patrol Craft Sailors Times."

PATROL CRAFT SAILORS TIMES
Too Good To Be Forgotten

c/o Wesley G. Johnson, 6484 Park Ave., Indianapolis 46220-1635 - Telephone: (317) 253-4801

Figure XII-2. This figure shows the masthead of one of the first issues of the "Patrol Craft Sailors Times" of the Patrol Craft Sailors Society started by Patrick Ward and Wesley G. Johnson.

In an article in an early issue of the "Patrol Craft Sailors Times" the leaders of the society wrote the following announcement to attract more members.

INTRODUCTION
     Our experience with sponsorship of the USS PC 564 Association and the USS PC 565 over some years has demonstrated the need for such an organization – and our mail tells us there exists an untold number of PC sailors who are unable to locate their buddies, or their unit, and as the years pass these unsatisfied yearnings are becoming more persistent and demanding. Time is growing short! We must do it now. This experience has moved us to do something about it. . . . will the readers of this newsletter please do what they can to help make this effort successful, spread the word, and support. Welcome aboard! Let us hear from you.
     THE PLAN
     The organization of a "Patrol Craft Sailors Society" to encompass all the sailors from PCs, PCEs, and SCs in the U. S. Navy – wartime and

peacetime – (WW II and Korea, Vietnam). The membership will require service as crew member from a qualified ship, which will be recognized as a warship, with anti-submarine, convoy, combat, and fleet connections for invasion forces, functions etc. We will have as our motto "We Were Too Good To Be Forgotten." We will spread the word among you with our periodic newsletter – "The Patrol Craft Sailors Times," soon to be printed and delivered with our mailing list attached. If we are successful in generating interest, we will sponsor a "Squadron Reunion" – in some convenient central location – say, like Omaha, Minneapolis, Chicago, St. Louis, Kansas City, Des Moines, Indianapolis – to be chosen by the popular will.

Later, the "Patrol Craft Sailors Times" contained an article stating that, because of increased interest in the organization, the Patrol Craft Sailors Society would be renamed the Patrol Craft Sailors Association (PCSA). This PCSA now has as its motto "Too Good To Be Forgotten."

Thanks to the foresight, imagination, and enthusiasm of Patrick Ward and Wesley Johnson the current Patrol Craft Sailors Association has more than 3,000 names of patrol craft, mine craft, and other small ship sailors in its roster. It maintains a website and publishes a "Newsletter." Since its first reunion in Jacksonville, Florida in March 1988 it has held annual reunions.

The PCSA established a museum/library/archive in Bay City, Michigan on 10 June 1994.[26]

The museum will preserve the history of patrol craft and small ship sailors of World War II, perpetuate their legacy, and provide information to users for future historical research.

The PCSA established its museum in Bay City, Michigan and held opening and dedication ceremonies for it in June 1994. For that occasion the government of the United States honored the Patrol Craft Sailors Association by having the United States Postal Service issue a First Day Cover. The cover has a picture of PC 1125 on it, and written on its face is an acknowledgment of Bay City, Michigan as the home of Patrol Craft Sailors. A replica of the first day cover is reproduced here.

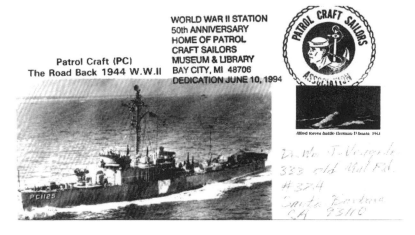

Figure XII-3. This United States Postal Service First Day Cover honors the dedication of the Patrol Craft Sailors Museum/Library/Archive on 10 June 1994 in Bay City, Michigan, the "birthplace" of PCs. It is addressed to the author and is from the author's collection.

The PCSA also has contributed money to the Navy Memorial in Washington, DC. Also it has installed an etched glass panel on the Grand Staircase in the Navy Memorial that shows a PC. It also sponsors a seat in the Arleigh and Roberta

Burke Theater in the Memorial.

The nationally announced and celebrated World War II Commemorative Community Program also bestowed another honor on the Patrol Craft Sailors Association in 1995. The Program, designed to honor those who served in World War II, invited the PCSA to become a member of the Commemorative Community Program. The Board of Directors and officers of the PCSA accepted the honor. The symbol of the organization is shown in the next figure.

Figure XII-4. This figure shows the World War II Commemorative Community Program Logo as accepted by the Patrol Craft Sailors Association. It is shown in color in the Section titled Color Plates. It is courtesy of the PCSA.

In its early days the PCSA started an open competition among its members to create a logo for the organization for use on stationery and other items. The response was large and varied. Some of the entries are shown on succeeding pages. They start with the theme from the poem "The PC Boat" by Melvin DeWitt, "Can you sit serene on a broncho (sic) mean, or stay on a plunging steer?" From there the theme seemed to encompass sea creatures. Finally the focus was on the men who sailed the ships. The final design selected and shown after the other entries was about The Man – The Sailor – The Swabbie – The White Hat. – the man who lugged a Sea Bag.

Figure XII-5. Proposed PCSA logo showing a wild bronco. It is courtesy of the Patrol Craft Sailors Association.

Figure XII-6. Proposed PCSA logo. This variation on the bronco theme uses a rampaging steer. It is courtesy of the Patrol Craft Sailors Association.

Figure XII-7. This proposed PCSA logo continues the rough rider theme but with nautical flavor using a dolphin. It is courtesy of the Patrol Craft Sailors Association.

Figure XII-8. This proposed PCSA logo is similar to the nautical rough rider theme with a porpoise. It is courtesy of the Patrol Craft Sailors Association.

Figure XII-9. In this proposed PCSA logo the rider becomes more daring on the back of an orca killer whale. It is courtesy of the Patrol Craft Sailors Association.

Figure XII-10. This proposed PCSA logo shows the rough rider on the back of a sword fish. It is courtesy of the Patrol Craft Sailors Association.

Figure XII-11. In this suggested PCSA logo the rough rider is a cartoon character on an unknown type of sea creature. It is courtesy of the Patrol Craft Sailors Association.

After a committee evaluated the many suggested logos they decided on a simpler one that focused not on an animal or sea creature but on a sailor. That one "white hat" represents all the men who went to sea during World War II on small ships. It is accompanied by the device that has appeared in many places over many years to typify naval activities and the naval establishment, a fouled anchor. Appropriately also, the adopted logo contains the important words from the first motto of the originally founded Patrol Craft Sailors Society that grew into the Patrol Craft Sailors Association.

For membership information about the PCSA contact Jim Heywood at jim.heywood@sdrc.com or at 7005 Bridges Road, Cincinnati, Ohio 45230.

Figure XII-12. This figure shows the finally adopted logo for the Patrol Craft Sailors Association. The PCSA uses it on stationery, the "Newsletter," official documents, and banners used to decorate areas where the organization holds meetings. It is courtesy of the Patrol Craft Sailors Association.

Small ship sailors spun many tales and recited many accounts about the way their ships took the seas. They told how their vessels flew from wave crests until much of their keels saw daylight and the ship hung there and quivered and bent hanging out of the water.

They told how the ships rode the crests of waves and then plunged into the troughs of towering waves that were higher than their masts. Green water roared back over the forecastle, pounded the pilot house, and swept back along the deck tearing at structures.

One Painting, by James F. Kennedy, that captured some of the essence of that action of a ship in a heavy sea flying over a large swell is presented next.

Figure XII-13. This figure is a black and white copy of James F. Kennedy's painting of PC 574. The painting helps establish the PC as Melvin DeWitt's poem, "The PC Boat," referred to it as a "Racing whippet and jumping goat – Leaping Lena, the PC boat." It is shown in color in the Section titled Color Plates. It is presented with the courtesy of the late James F. Kennedy.

Copies of other paintings by James Kennedy are shown in the next three figures and in the section titled Color Plates

Figure XII-14. James Kennedy painted this aerial view of a PC. It is shown in color in the Section titled Color Plates. It is courtesy of the late James Kennedy.

Figure XII-15. This painting was titled "Moonlight Convoy." It is shown in color in the Section titled Color Plates. It is courtesy of the late James Kennedy

Figure XII-16. This painting was titled "In Port for R & R." It is shown in color in the Section titled Color Plates. It is courtesy of the late James Kennedy

While in the naval service many men aboard the small ships created handcrafted items such as ash trays, jewelry, belt buckles, knife handles, etc. Some men continued this activity after they returned home from the war and produced items with nautical themes or that were made from nautical gear. Shown are two examples of this type of hand crafts.

Figure XII-17. The lamps are made from different shells. The bottom is from a 3"-50 shell. The base is part of the casing, cut and flattened. Above that is the base of the same shell that contained the detonator. There are four 30.06 shells for legs, and between them are four 45 cal. rounds. In the middle is a 20 mm shell to which the light is attached. On the pull chain is a carbine bullet. The lamp was made by, and the photograph is courtesy of Jacob VanBelkum who served as a Gunner's Mate on PC 793.

Figure XII-18. The bottom of the picture frame is wood on top of which is a 20 mm shell cut in half lengthways and welded together. On top of that are two 30.06 and two carbine shells. The frame is made of two pieces of metal with plastic in between to cover the picture. It can be flipped over to show a picture on either side. The girl in the picture is one Jacob dated in high school, wrote to while he was in service, and now for fifty-six years has been his wife. The picture frame was made by and the photograph is courtesy of Jacob VanBelkum.

Another motif used by many men for handcrafted items they made that recalled their days aboard small ships was the ship's wheel, its helm. In port the bridge was a favorite hangout space where men could exchange scuttlebutt. The helm was a focal point in the bridge. At sea it was the center of attention, guiding the ship on its course.

One man recreated a ship's wheel from miscellaneous parts to help himself and his family remember World War II and his duty on a small ship.

Figure XII-19. This ship's wheel was made from an old necktie rack, file handles for spokes, a train whistle that looked like a Boatswain's pipe, hammer handle to represent an SP's billy club, and a clock. The wheel is shown in the Section titled Color Plates. It was made by and is courtesy of Donald R. Hatfield.

Ship modeling has always been a favorite pastime of sailors, and it was the same with the small ship sailors of World War II. During their wartime days they did not have the tools, parts, and time to build models. And constructing a replica of a United States Navy or Coast Guard vessel was a breach of wartime security. Modelers had to wait until after the war to practice their hobby, and they did. Models of small ships are almost all that remains of the ships and, therefore, these models are important historical artifacts. Photographs of a few of them are shown on the following four pages.

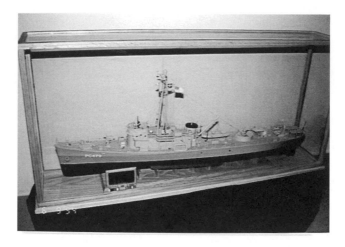

Figure XII-20. Model of PC 479 at the Patrol Craft Sailors Association Museum. Thomas A. Pollock built the model. The photograph is from the author's collection.

Figure XII-21. Charles P. Turner built this model of SC 1287 from scratch to 1/32" scale from his own plans. Most of the parts were hand made, and the model is radio controlled. The photograph is courtesy of Charles P. Turner.

Figure XII-22. This is a photograph of the model of YMS 307 built from original prints to 3/8 scale. The Rice Brothers Corp. Built YMS ships during the war. The photograph is courtesy of Robert B. Rice.

Figure XII-23. Theodore Treadwell commissioned Fine Arts Models to build this model of SC 648. He deeded the model to the Navy Museum in Washington, D. C. A color picture is in the Section titled Color Plates. The photograph is courtesy of Ted Treadwell.

Figure XII-24. Joe Kelliher started this model as PC 1122. Tom Pollock finished it as PGM 18. A color photograph is in the Section titled Color Plates. The photograph is courtesy of Bob Daly.

Figure XII-25. This 1" to 10' model of YP 478 was made by James H. Byington. It is shown in color in the Section titled Color Plates. Property of the Bay County Historical Society, used with permission.

Figure XII-26. This nineteen inch long model of PCE 847 is of an unique ship. It was one of two PCEs converted to weather ships. It was made in the 1980s from Lindberg AM kits by Frank G. Soulier. The photograph is courtesy of, Frank G. Soulier.

Besides hand crafts and ship modeling many men continued with their other talents and methods of self expression after their discharge from the service. Some of them developed latent aptitudes for creativity that they knew existed. Others discovered that they had gifts or abilities of which they had not been unaware.

Many men generated and had published written works in journals, magazines, and newsletters, and they wrote fiction and nonfiction books. The "Newsletter" of the Patrol Craft Sailors Association, for example, contains many written accounts of exploits of small ships and their crew members, written by the men who served on the ships. Their narratives make the issues of the "Newsletter" an important historical collection. A few of the books written by former "Donald Duck Navy" sailors are listed in the Bibliography. All the written works these men generated are too numerous to list here, and they are too lengthy to include in this book, but they offer historians and other interested persons a large collection of personal observations of the years of World War II at sea.

Graphic arts, cartooning, and painting became hobbies and vocations for some of the former sailors. In many instances their output was related to or reminiscent of their naval service or generally about World War II. Also they contributed their talents to various Navy, Coast Guard, veteran, and patriotic association magazines and news papers.

Representative examples of this post-war creativity of writing, painting, and other activities that are reminiscent of or related to the Navy or the United States are given in this section.

Figure XII-27. This black and white copy of a painting by Joe Luca, who served on PC 780, shows a PC bearing down on and ready to ram a surfaced German U-boat during the Battle of the Atlantic. He made the painting in 1950 with tempera water based sign paint on cardboard. It was his rendition of a cover on a 1944 edition of Yachting Magazine. A color copy is in the Section titled Color Plates. It is courtesy of Joe Luca.

Not all ships' insignia were cartoons. Some men used military and patriotic motifs such as that shown next.

U.S.S PC 1178

Figure XII-28. This Signet, was drawn by William Tormey in memory of his ship. It is shown in color in the Section titled Color Plates. The Signet is courtesy of William Tormey.

Most of all, these erstwhile young men who sailed and fought the small ships in World War II did so with pride, honor, and patriotism. In their later years they maintained those characteristics. Today, as their numbers decrease, they continue to feel the same emotions they experienced in their youth and they continue to show pride in their service, the young men who serve now, and their country. These attitudes are illustrated in the following two selections. The first one considers the relationship between old and new sailors.

OF WOODEN SHIPS AND IRON MEN

The Wooden Ships, of days gone by
Are still appealing to the eye.

Where are the Sailors who manned those ships?
Today they can only be seen in movie "clips."

The Ships of today are dressed in Steel
But the Love, the Warmth, you still can feel.

You may change their structure; even their names
Why have we never, ever, changed their "Games."

The Sailors of today, their deep desire
Continues, as always, to inspire.

Some journeys are longer, nay, further across the Sea yes,
Lonely, forbidding to you and to me.

Yet, through the years, tradition to carry on
Our Sailors have proved; they ARE made of IRON.

Now as you sight them, in their "Whites" or "Blues" Among the
world's best they're yours to choose.

For when this world is done with them
Its only in Heaven we will surely find
The IRON MEN.

This poem was written by Jack Hogan on 7 June 1999

The next poem, by W. C. Moore illustrates the old
sailor's patriotism and reverence for the symbol of our country.

IT HAS EARNED IT'S DUE

With it's red and white stripes a flying
Flashing fifty sparkling white stars on a blue field close
to the pole
This is our flag – our symbol – "Old Glory – our
country's soul.

It has earned it's keep o'er two hundred years
Proudly flying amongst laughter and tears
Waving to and for – the whole wide world to know

She has sheltered multitudes with uncontrolled and uncountable fears.

This banner is continually wind whipped from morn till night
Announcing to the world's populace to hear
This country was founded for rights and right – not might
Allowing all – the freedom of words, and deeds, not fright.

Do not ever think of maltreating me
Burning and/or desecrating is sacrilegious and sad
It ignites five alarm fires from all who served her true
Those who fought tirelessly for our country's banner
The red white & blue.

Freedom's land stretches from east to west
Bounded by the Atlantic to the east – Pacific way out west
Three thousand miles of valleys, prairies, and mountains peaks
Sheltering men and women of every race creed and color
Mattering little as to the language   each speaks.

Guiding our men and women through special events and peaceful times
Solidifying unity and spirit – real American spirit
Especially when wars – those man-made hells unfold.

This banner we honor this day used to hang on school room walls
We'd spot it every morn
Awaiting those few special and almost reverent words
I pledge allegiance to the flag.

Bill Moore concluded his poem by voicing the sentiment of many veterans of World War II when he wrote:

"Our forefathers memorized this verse
We their survivors love this country like they
We must re-institute this tradition."

The poem and sentiment above, written on 29 October 2000, is by and courtesy of William C. Moore.

An emotion experienced by former sailors is that of nostalgia for the days of youth and recognition that they are gone; replaced by the calmer benefits of The Later Years.

TO ALL THE SMALL CRAFT SAILORS

We who were young and are old,
who were foolish and are sensible,
who gutted the years recklessly and now
number the days in wisdom,
who desperately clasped girls
and now fondly cherish wives:
Open the closed books, wake the memories,
sniff the sea breezes of nostalgia,
and then let us fill a cup
and drink with love to that most noble,
ridiculous, laughable, sublime,
departed figure in all our lives –
The Young Sailor that was each of us.
Let us drink to his dreams
for they were rainbow-hued;
to his appetites for they were strong;
to his blunders for they were huge;
to his beloved for she was sweet;
to his pain for it was sharp;
to his time for it was brief;

and to his end for it was to become one of us.
And in that land of memory where the sun never fades,
where the flowers are spring flowers and
the grass Is an April green forever --
he still walks his jaunty, infinitely optimistic, enthusiastic way.

May the good Lord maintain some of this in us today

The small ship sailor author of this poem and sentiment is unknown. It is courtesy of Ted Treadwell.

It was more than sixty years ago that thousands of young men entered the sea services of the United States to fight in World War II. Those erstwhile young men are now in their later years. Just as they displayed honor, devotion to duty, courage, and even humor in pursuing the war then, they continued to show these traits later in civilian life. It was no wonder they became part of what is known as "The Greatest Generation." Even now they continue to show those same remarkable characteristics.

During the war they displayed many of their feelings and emotions through art, crafts, writing, and humor. Samples of their work are in preceding chapters. Since World War II many of them continued to show their originality, illustrations of which are given in this chapter.

The sad fact is, though, that because of increasing age and diminishing health, some of those men no longer can demonstrate their creative abilities. They may no longer be the young sailor who, as described in the poem above, "walks his jaunty, infinitely optimistic, enthusiastic way."

These now older men can no longer generate the wonderful items they had created for so many years. Sadder still is the realization that within a few decades all their thoughts, voices, pens, and hands will be forever stilled. Only memories of those young, "jaunty, infinitely optimistic" men will persist in the minds of those who knew them and by the works they left such as the items collected in this book.

But – as Ted Treadwell wrote in the Dedication in his book *Splinter Fleet* – "To the brave young men who served in the Splinter Fleet – and especially those who did not return."

Though shattered planks 'neath oceans lie,
Their souls in peace shall never die.

EPILOGUE

Like the ships, the young men who served on them also are disappearing into the depths of history. Various types of United States Navy and Coast Guard combat ships participated in World War II. After the war some of them continued to serve. Others became target ships and followed many of their less fortunate sister vessels to the bottom of the oceans. Hundreds of ships fell to welders' torches and became scrap to be used in peaceful applications.

Government agencies and some private organizations preserved a few representatives of most of the types of United States ships. They now are museums, some afloat some landlocked. They are available for former sailors and their families and future generations of people to visit and learn what it was like to be a sailor in World War II.

While aboard any of these museum ships people see and touch the cold steel of the vessel. They pass through the bridge and hear, in their mind's ears, orders to maneuver and operate the ship. In the officer's wardroom they stare at the green felt table where officers ate and conferred, and they see ship's items, personal trinkets; old flags; and other memorabilia. Passing through the mess hall they visualize young men balancing and grasping at their meals as the ship rolled and pitched. In the crowded living compartments they picture men in body-wide triple layer bunks with a thin mattress and two wool blankets grasping what sleep they could between grueling watches. In the bowels of the ship, the engine room, their ears seem drowned in the pounding of engines and whining of machinery, and they feel the blasting heat. At the gun stations they stare along gun muzzles as kamikazes plunge toward them. They hear the whine and thud of bullets and shrapnel tearing into the flesh of shipmates. All this visitors can do and sense what it was like to serve on and be at war on a naval ship.

Mostly though these visitors can do this only for the larger ships. Years after the war, people rushed to preserve the battleships, cruisers, destroyers, submarines, and other large vessels. Not much energy, time, or money became available for doing the same thing for the small ships, however. Of the thousands of patrol and mine craft, Cutters, and similar small ships that fought the war only one remains as a monument to the entire Donald Duck Navy – the minesweeper, USS *Hazard* AM 240. Almost as another show of lack of interest in and a last indignity to the small ship fleet, their only representative, USS *Hazard*, does not roll freely in the waters in which she fought. Instead she lies buried halfway to her gunwales in earth in Omaha, Nebraska.

Except for that lone ship, now and for the future, people can learn what it was like on a small United States combatant only through old black and white photographs, a few feet of decaying movie film, video tapes, internet websites, and a few books. The films known to the author are listed in the section titled Film Library, and the websites and books are listed in the Sections titled Related Websites and Bibliography.

But what of the young men who sailed across the oceans, lived their lives, and fought the enemy on those ships? From images staring up from the pages of old photograph albums, we, and future generations, can see what those men – boys, many not old enough to drink alcohol, drive a motor vehicle, or vote – looked like. We see what they wore, and how they smiled and laughed at their confined, boring, and dangerous duty.

There is some record, however, of what they thought and said, and did. This comes mostly from recollections composed years after the fact from memories. Whatever exists in writing from the time they were aboard ship is primarily in letters they wrote home. But these letters are truncated by censorship so we cannot always understand the true stories of what the men were trying to say.

In many ways, what they wanted to say was expressed better in their creations, their poems, their pictures, their cartoons. Much of it was lost or lays neglected in family archives. A small amount has been made public, and some is recorded in this book. I hope the samples shown here revive memories of the days aboard ship for the young men who were there and enlightens other readers about the life they led.

Over more than half a century since World War II, some of these erstwhile young men and boys have continued to generate memories through their continuing art works. Some of their work also is in this book. I hope it shows the emotional attachment small ship sailors had to their country, their duty, their experiences, and their shipmates.

Over the next few decades their voices, pens, and brushes will be stilled. Small ship sailors of the future, and the world, will have lost a precious resource. But they will have gained an equally precious legacy – the creative works of the men of the "Donald Duck Navy" who were "Too Good To Be Forgotten."

APPENDIX A

ITEMS ISSUED TO AN ENLISTED MAN

On entering Boot Camp, besides getting his shots and a buzz haircut, a Navy recruit discarded his civilian attire and possessions and received the uniforms and other gear he would use during his period of enlistment.

He needed a place to store these items, so one of the first items issued to him was his Sea Bag. This cylindrical canvas sack of 26" x 36" had grommets on top through which the man wove a line to use as a draw string to close the bag and to hang it from a rack. As with everything else he got, he stenciled his name on the side of the bag. This Sea Bag was his and his only. It was his entire and unique identity as an individual among the mass of other men.

Next came uniforms that the recruit learned to fold, roll, and store in the Sea Bag. Then the Navy provided him a device for his sleep. In the tradition of the old navy they issued him a hammock with a mattress, two mattress covers (sailors called them fart sacks), one pillow, two pillow covers, and two blankets.

When traveling, a sailor rolled the mattress and sleeping gear inside the hammock which he then wrapped around and secured to his Sea Bag. This pack he slung up on a shoulder and marched off with all he owned.[27]

Figure A-1. This picture is of a typical Sea Bag used by the United States Navy and Coast Guard enlisted men during World War II. Men kept everything they owned in it when traveling or at temporary stations. Aboard ship they moved its contents into a locker. This is a U. S. Navy photograph.

Before rolling his mattress a man laid out his bedding items on the flattened mattress in a specific order according to regulations. The order was not arbitrary. It came from much experience and resulted in a compact package when rolled.

Figure A-2. This photograph shows a Boot's hammock laid flat with his mattress, blankets, and pillow displayed in proper order. It shows how the lines for hanging the hammock were coiled inside the package. The photograph was from a card given to recruits. It is from the author's collection.

Sailors did not just stuff their clothing into their Sea Bag. It had to be prepared first according to regulations and then inserted in a particular order. This procedure insured first that the clothing would take up a minimum of space so it would all fit in the Sea Bag. Secondly by rolling items and tying them they tended to have fewer wrinkles when unrolled.

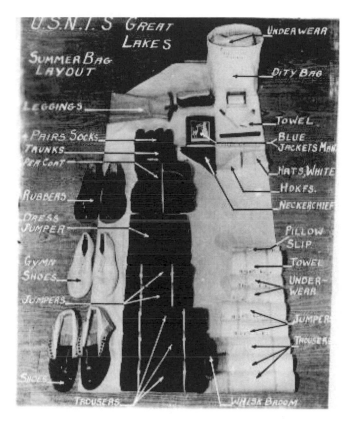

Figure A-3. This photograph shows the contents of a Boot's Sea Bag laid out for inspection. Note how all items of clothing are rolled and tied. The photograph is from a post card the author sent from Co. 305, U. S. Naval Training Station, Great Lakes, Illinois to his family on 7 April 1943. It is from the author's collection.

    Finally the moment came when a new sailor had his mattress rolled and Sea Bag full. Then he formed the rolled mattress around the Sea Bag and restrained it with a line. Then proudly, with a grunt because of its weight, he swung it up and balanced it on his shoulder. At that moment he marched off to his next assignment. On many occasions it was to clamber aboard one of the ships of the "Donald Duck Navy."

    Figure A-4. Here we see a sailor in a World War II poster warning people to not disclose fleet information. He is carrying his Sea Bag and hammock. By the end of his cruise his Sea Bag will be filled with memories. The picture is from the National Archives and Records Administration.

APPENDIX B

PHOTOGRAPHS OF SMALL SHIPS

This appendix contains at least one photograph of each type of ship discussed in this book. These items are not meant to be a complete catalog of the ships. They are, however, representative of them. Most ships of any type were arranged in classes, and their features, including engines, armament, deck gear, etc. varied between classes. Even in one particular class of vessel the features varied from ship to ship.

For more photographs of small ships the reader is referred to the other books listed in the Bibliography near the end of this book. Numerous websites also display photographs of various United States Navy and Coast Guard ships. Some of these websites are given in the Section titled Related Websites.

PC Patrol Craft

Figure B-1. This photograph of PC 799, c.1944, is from the Navsource website and was enhanced by Tom Kermen. It is U.S. Navy Photo NH 85155 of the Naval Historical Center.

Figure B-2. This photograph shows PC 823 in "Dressed Ship" status to celebrate VJ Day on 14 August 1945. The photograph is courtesy of Elmer G. Muth.

PGM Motor Gunboat ex PC

Figure B-3. This photograph of PGM 29 is from the Navsource website. It is there courtesy of Bob Daly.

AM Minesweeper ex PC

Figure B-4. AM 90 (PC-1594) off the Norfolk Navy Yard, Virginia, on 4 June 1944. This USN Photograph 96494 is from the Navsource website.

PCE Patrol Craft Escort

Figure B-5. This photograph of PCE 845, of the PCE 842 class, is courtesy of Tom Kermen and is from the Navsource website.

AM Minesweeper (Similar to a PCE)

Figure B-6. This photograph shows Admirable class USS *Hazard*, AM 240 a museum ship, land-locked in Freedom Park in Omaha, Nebraska. It is a United States Navy photograph from the Navsource website

SC Submarine Chaser

Figure B-7. This photograph of SC 1009, of the SC 497 class, is from the website of the Patrol Craft Sailors Association.

PGM Motor Gunboat ex SC

Figure B-8. This picture of PGM 6, ex SC 1071, was photographed in January 1944. It is U.S. Navy photograph NH 96496 from the Naval Historical Center and the Hyperwar website.

PCS Patrol Craft Sweeper

Figure B-9. This photograph of PCS 1402 is from the Navsource website. It was taken on D Day, Okinawa, September 1945 in Hagushi Harbor, western side. It is courtesy of Bill Kinney and E J Comeau.

YMS Auxiliary Motor Minesweeper

Figure B-10. This photograph of YMS 44 is from the Hyperwar website.

YP, PY, and PYc ex Yachts

Figure B-11. This is a 1944 picture of YP 611 (ex yacht *Jordano*). She joined the U. S. Navy in 1943 and was struck from the list in 1946. Conrad Brown still operates her as the excursion boat, *Black Tie*, in Florida. A photograph of the *Black Tie* is shown in Chapter X. The photograph is courtesy of Conrad Brown.

Figure B-12. PY 14 *Argus* was built in 1929 as steel-hulled yacht *Haida* in Germany. The Navy acquired her on 25 October 1940 and commissioned her on 12 February 1941. The photograph is circa 1944/1945 and is courtesy of Warren A. Cabral and Todd Cabral.

Figure B-13. PYc 26 was built in 1926 as the yacht *Robador.* The Navy acquired her on 2 March 1942 and commissioned her USS *Cymophane* (PYc-26) on 6 August 1942. The photograph is from the Navsource website.

U. S. Coast Guard Cutters

Figure B-14. This photograph is of the 165' USCG *Calypso,* WPC-104. It was taken from the Navsource website.

Figure B-15. This photograph is of the U. S. Coast Guard 125' Cutter *Cuyahoga* WSC 157. The ship is ready to depart from the Coast Guard Yard in Curtis Bay, Maryland on 11 February 1945. The photograph is courtesy of Joseph G. Hoff.

APPENDIX C

SPECIFICATIONS OF SMALL SHIPS

The descriptions and specifications for the ships given here are not universal but are typical for each type or a class of ship. The specifications listed are not necessarily for the particular ships whose photographs are shown in Appendix B. They are for ships of the class.

For more specifications and more general information on small ships the reader is referred to other books that are listed in the Bibliography near the end of this book.

Numerous internet websites also contain specifications for various United States Navy and Coast Guard ships. Some of these websites are given in the Section titled Related Websites.

PC Patrol Craft

These ships, designed in four classes, were steel hulled, 173' long, 450 ton, Diesel propelled. They were typically armed with a 3"-50 gun, 40-mm and 20-mm machine guns, K-guns for depth charges, depth charge racks, and mousetraps. The United States Navy had constructed 361 ships on the PC hull design at sixteen shipyards. Some of these ships the Navy converted to mine sweepers (AM) and gunboats (PGM). Information on them is given in this Appendix. Further information about the PC, AM, and PGM ships is in books listed in the Bibliography.

PC Patrol Craft Specifications of the PC 461 Class:(219 PCs were commissioned)
Steel hulls
Length Overall: 173' 8"
Extreme Beam: 23'
Displacement: 284 tons. Displacement on Load Draft: 360 tons. Full Load Displacement: 450 tons
Maximum Draft: 10' 10"
Average Draft: 7'
Endurance: 3,000 Nautical Miles at 12 knots.
Armament: One 3"-50 caliber gun, one single 40-mm Bofors machine gun, five 20-mm Oerlikon machine guns, two forward throwing mousetraps, two K-guns, and two stern mounted depth charge racks
Designed Speed: 20.2 knots
Flank Speed: 21 knots
Gyrocompass: Sperry, Mark XIV, Model 1.
Fuel Capacity: 20,378 gallons
Lubricating Oil Capacity: 2,942 gallons
Fresh Water Capacity: 4,386 gallons

Propellers: Two, Bronze, 72" diameter, three blades.
Engines: Two Diesels, Directly reversible. Types used were:

Fairbanks Morse & Co. Model 38D-a, two stroke cycle, 10 cylinder, opposed piston. (PC 461-470, 483-487, 563-572, 578-582, 600-603, 616-619, 1077-1082, 1176-1180, 1231-1233, 1251-1254, 1260-1263).

General Motors Corp. Model 16-2588-A, four stroke cycle, 16 cylinder, "V" type. (PC 471-479, 548-560, 583-590, 596-599, 606, 620-623, 1086-1149, 1167-1175, 1225-1230, 1241-1247, 1546-1569).

Hooven, Owens, Rentshler Co. (H.O.R.) Model 9DA-A, two stroke cycle, double acting, 9 cylinder (The remainder of the PCs).

Shafts: Two. One hydraulic coupling and reduction gear on each shaft.
Shaft Horsepower: 2,280 Horsepower
Auxiliary Engines: Two Diesels. Ships with F. M. or G. M. engines used the G. M. Model 6-71. Ships with H. O. R. engines used Buda Model 6DHG-691 Diesel engines. All ships used two 60-kilowatt, 120 volt direct current generator sets.

PGM Motor Gunboat ex PC

These ships had the same internal configuration as the PCs, but their armor and armament differed. They had an armor plated open bridge and armor plates along the hull over the fuel tanks and engine room. Also, the antisubmarine gear and weapons were removed.

PGM Specifications for PGM 12, ex PC 1088 (The Navy converted 24 PC hulls to PGMs)
Displacement: 295 tons full load

Length: 175'
Beam: 23'
Draft: 10' 10"
Speed: 20 knots
Complement: 59 officers and enlisted men
Armament: One twin 40-mm gun mount, six 20-mm, one twin .50 cal. machine gun, one 60-mm mortar.
Propulsion: Two General Motors 16-278A diesel engines, two shafts.

AM Minesweeper ex PC

The internal configuration was similar to that on PCs, except that they used different kinds of Diesel engines and their deck gear differed. Trawl gear was added near the depth charge racks. The ships proved inadequate as minesweepers and the Navy reconverted them into PCs.

AM ex PC Specifications (18 were converted from PC hulls)
Similar to PC specifications except for trawl gear aft
Some AMs used Cooper Bessemer or Alco Diesel engines.
Specifications here are for AM 90.
Displacement: 295 tons
Length: 173'
Beam: 23'
Draft: 11' 7"
Speed: 17 knots
Complement: 65 officers and enlisted men
Armament: one single 3"-50 gun mount, one single 40-mm gun mount; three 20-mm guns, two rocket launchers, four depth charge projectiles, two depth charge racks.
Propulsion: Two Cooper-Bessemer GNB-8 diesel engines, two shafts.

PCE Patrol Craft Escort

When the United States entered World War II it needed escort vessels. The Navy built PCs and SCs until it could build larger ships. The next type was the PCE. Longer than a PC it had a broader beam and larger tonnage. PCEs carried detection and ranging gear for locating submarines. Some PCEs were converted to PCER, Patrol Craft Escort Rescue. Some others became amphibious control vessels, PCEC. Two PCEs became weather ships.

PCE Patrol Craft Escort Specifications (63 were built)
Steel hulls
Specifications here are for PCE 845.
Length: 184' 6"
Beam: 33'1"
Draft: 9' 8"
Displacement: 903 tons full load
Speed: 16 knots
Engines: GM Diesel 12-278A, 2000 Shaft Horse Power
Complement: 9 officers, 90 enlisted men
Armament: One 3"-50, three 40-mm Bofors, five 20-mm Oerlikons, Hedgehog, four depth charge throwers, two depth charge racks
Propulsion: Two Diesel engines.

AM Fleet Minesweeper (Similar to a PCE)

These ships used the same hull, engines, and superstructure as the PCE. The fantail was modified for mine sweep gear including davits and winches for streaming sweep gear. To accommodate this gear, the aft gun tub on the PCE design was removed and replaced by two twin 40-mm gun tubs on the aft end of the main deck.

AM Minesweeper (PCE type) Specifications (121 were built)
Displacement: 650 tons
Length: 184' 6"
Beam: 33'
Draft: 9' 9"
Speed: 14.8 knots
Complement: 11 officers, 93 enlisted men
Fuel capacity: 1,050 barrels
Armament: One 3"-50 gun, two twin 40-mm, Hedgehog, depth charge racks.

SC Submarine Chaser

These wooden-hulled ships were designed for coastal patrols and for anti-submarine warfare starting with the Nazi U-Boat menace along the Atlantic seaboard. Later the Navy used them for convoy escort and many other duties. The SCs also became amphibious landing control ships used during invasions.

SC Subchaser Specifications (438 were built)
Wooden hulls
These specifications are for SC 1009.
Length Overall:110' 10"
Extreme Beam: 17' 11.5"
Displacement: 98 Tons
Maximum Draft full load: 6' 6"
Speed: 15.6 knots or 21 knots depending on engines used
Complement: 3 officers, 24 enlisted men
Armament: One Single 3"-50 or one single 40-mm Bofor, one or two twin mount .50-cal machine gun(s), two or three K Guns, 14 Depth Charges with six single release chocks, two

sets of MK 20 Mousetrap rails with four 7.2 projectiles
Propulsion: Two 880 hp General Motors 8-268A or two 1,540
HP General Motors 16-184A "pancake" diesel engines, two
shafts
Endurance: 1,500 nautical miles at 12 knots

PGM Motor Gunboat ex SC

Because PT boats used for in-shore patrol had limited range and firepower, the Navy converted some SCs to gunboats. They had similar construction and configuration as SCs, but the engines were the pancake type. The designers replaced the SC pilot house with an open cockpit, and added a folding radar mast. Additional armor was placed around gun stations. The armament of the PGM differed from an SC armament as shown here.

PGM, ex SC 1071 Specifications (8 were converted from SC hulls)
Wooden hulls
Displacement: 95 tons
Length: 110'
Beam: 23'
Draft: 10' 10"
Speed: estimated at 21 knots
Complement: 50 officers and enlisted men
Armament: One single 3"-50, two twin 40-mm Bofors, six 20-mm Oerlikons, one twin .50 cal. machine gun, one 60-mm Mortar
Engines: Two General Motors 16-184A "pancake" diesel engines with 1540 BHP.

PCS Patrol Craft Sweeper

The Navy used these ships for submarine patrol and mine sweeping. Also, because of their small size some became school ships for training enlisted men and officers who would man patrol and mine sweeper type ships.

PCS Patrol Craft Sweeper Specifications (59 were built)
Wooden hulls
Length: 136'
Beam: 24' 6"
Displacement: 251 tons
Draft: 8' 7"
Engines: Two geared diesel engines, 900 Brake Horse Power
Speed: 14 knots
Endurance: 3,000 nautical miles at 12 knots
Complement: 57 enlisted men and officers
Armament: Main Battery One 3"-50, one 40-mm Bofors, two 20-mm Oerlikons, four K-gun depth charge throwers.

YMS Auxiliary Motor Minesweeper

The wooden hulled YMS was a durable and versatile type ship originally designed and used for inshore mine sweeping including at amphibious landing sites. They also performed many other functions. They had the same general characteristics but varied somewhat in appearance.

YMS Auxiliary Motor Minesweeper Specifications (561 were built)
Wooden hulls
Displacement: 320 tons (full displacement)
Length: 136'
Beam: 24'6"

Draft: 6'1"
Speed: 13 knots
Armament: One 3"-50, two 20-mm Oerlikons, two depth charge racks plus two extensions, two depth charge throwers
Complement: 4 officers, 29 enlisted men
Engines: Two General Motors Diesel engines, 500 HP.

PY and PYc ex Yachts

These vessels were mostly private yachts their owners donated to or were appropriated by the U. S. Navy. They were so varied that a single description does not fit them. Information on them may be found in books in the Bibliography and the Related Websites.

Specifications for PY 14 USS *Argus*
Displacement: 859 tons
Length: 207' 6"
Beam: 30'
Draft: 13' 5"
Speed: 13.5 knots
Complement: 59 officers and enlisted men
Armament: one 3"-50 gun
Propulsion: two 750HP Krupp diesel engines.

Specifications for PYc 28 USS Ability.
Displacement: 241 tons
Length: 133'
Beam: 21' 6"
Draft: 8'
Speed: 13 knots
Complement: 43 officers and enlisted men
Armament: One 20-mm gun.

YP Yard Patrol

These vessels were of numerous types and sizes. The Navy used them for harbor patrol and miscellaneous duties. No one type fits all those in use during World War II.

United States Coast Guard Cutters

A Cutter was defined as a U. S. Coast Guard vessel of 65 feet or more in length that has a designated commanding officer and living accommodations aboard for the crew. During World War II the Coast Guard operated various size Cutters. Many of them can be considered small ocean going ships, and they all made significant contributions to the war. I acknowledge and pay tribute to all of them but select two types as representative of all Cutters. Those of special interest as patrol and antisubmarine type Cutters considered in this book are the 165 foot WPC and the 125 foot WSC.

Cutters built before WWII and designated WPC

These were one of the more important Coast Guard subchasers. The United States built them during the Prohibition era to interdict smugglers. They also were used on ice patrol. Later the Navy converted them into subchasers.

Specifications for the 165' US Coast Guard Cutter type designated WPC
Steel hull
Cost: $258,000 each
Displacement: (tons) 337 full load (1934); 350 fullload (1945)
Length: 165'
Beam: 25' 3"
Draft: 7' 8" trial (1931); 7' max (1934); 10' max (1945)

Main Engines: 2 Winton, 6-cyl. Model 158 diesels
BHP: 1,340
Propellers: Twin, 3 blades
Performance: Maximum Speed:16.0 knots on trial (1931)
Maximum sustained speed: 14.0 knots for a 1,750 mile radius (1945)
Cruising: 11.0 knots, 3,000 mile radius (1945)
Economic: 6.0 knots, 6,417 mile radius (1945)
Diesel (95%): 7,700 gallons
Complement: (1945) 5 officers, 39 enlisted men (1938); 7 officers, 68 enlisted men (1945)
Armament:1932 and 1938: one 3"-23, two one-pounders. 1941: one 3"-23, one Y-gun, two depth charge racks. 1945: two 3"-50, two 20-mm, two depth charge racks, two Y-guns, two Mousetraps.

Cutters built before WWII and designated WSC

These were another important type of Coast Guard subchasers. The United States built them during the Prohibition era to interdict smugglers. Later the Navy converted them into subchasers.

Specifications for the 125' US Coast Guard Cutter type designated WSC

Steel hull
Displacement: 85 tons full load (1917); 167 tons full load (1943)
Length: 110'
Beam: 14' 9"
Draft: 5' 8" (1917)
Main Engines: Three Standard Motor Construction Co., 6 cyl gasoline

Horsepower: 600 SHP
Propellers: Triple
Performance: Maximum speed18.0 knots in design (1918).
Maximum sustained speed 14.0 knots, 680 mile radius
(1942). Cruising speed 11 knots, 760 mile radius (1942)
Complement: 2 officers, 25 enlisted men (1917)
Armament: 1917 one 3"-23, two 30-cal machine guns, one
DCP (Y-gun), 1943: one 3"-23, two 30-cal machine guns,
two mousetraps, two depth charge racks.

PLATES

ENGINEERING DRAWINGS
OF A PC

Robert Baldwin, then a nineteen-year-old sailor on PC 543 during World War II, walked the entire ship with a tape measure, pencil, and sketch pad. He searched every area and compartment and sketched and recorded details of the ship with their measurements, except the engine rooms. After discharge from the Navy, years later, he converted his sketches to the thirty engineering drawings shown in this appendix. The Plates are numbered 1 through 30. Number 20 is not used in the set, but there is a Supplemental Plate that shows the starboard exterior of the superstructure of a PC.

A set of blueprints for plan and elevation views and external and internal details of a PC is available from John Tombaugh, 5009 W. Beaman Lane, Rochester, IN 46975.

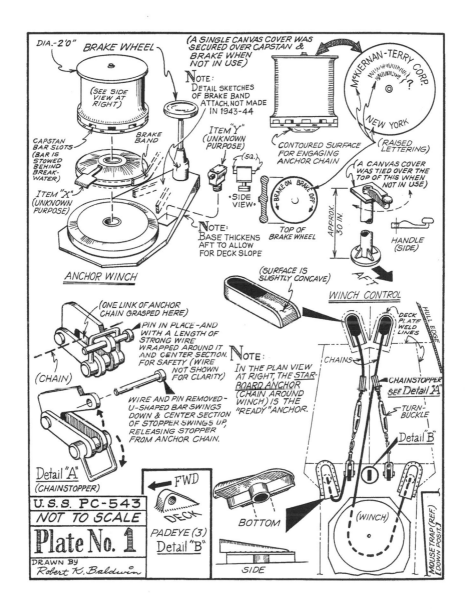

DIA.-2'0" BRAKE WHEEL

(A SINGLE CANVAS COVER WAS SECURED OVER CAPSTAN & BRAKE WHEN NOT IN USE)

McKIERNAN-TERRY CORP.

(SEE SIDE VIEW AT RIGHT)

NOTE: DETAIL SKETCHES OF BRAKE BAND ATTACH. NOT MADE IN 1943-44

NEW YORK

(RAISED LETTERING)

CAPSTAN BAR SLOTS (BAR IS STOWED BEHIND BREAKWATER)

BRAKE BAND

ITEM "Y" (UNKNOWN PURPOSE)

(SQ.)

CONTOURED SURFACE FOR ENGAGING ANCHOR CHAIN

(A CANVAS COVER WAS TIED OVER THE TOP OF THIS WHEN NOT IN USE)

SIDE VIEW

BRAKE ON BRAKE OFF

ITEM "X" (UNKNOWN PURPOSE)

NOTE: BASE THICKENS AFT TO ALLOW FOR DECK SLOPE

TOP OF BRAKE WHEEL

APPROX. 30 IN.

HANDLE (SIDE)

ANCHOR WINCH

(SURFACE IS SLIGHTLY CONCAVE)

AFT

WINCH CONTROL

(ONE LINK OF ANCHOR CHAIN GRASPED HERE)

PIN IN PLACE - AND WITH A LENGTH OF STRONG WIRE WRAPPED AROUND IT AND CENTER SECTION. FOR SAFETY (WIRE NOT SHOWN FOR CLARITY)

DECK PLATE WELD LINES

HULL EDGE

(CHAIN)

NOTE: IN THE PLAN VIEW AT RIGHT, THE STARBOARD ANCHOR (CHAIN AROUND WINCH) IS THE "READY" ANCHOR.

CHAINS

CHAINSTOPPER SEE Detail "A"

WIRE AND PIN REMOVED - U-SHAPED BAR SWINGS DOWN & CENTER SECTION OF STOPPER SWINGS UP, RELEASING STOPPER FROM ANCHOR CHAIN.

TURN-BUCKLE

Detail "B"

Detail "A" (CHAINSTOPPER)

FWD

U.S.S. PC-543

NOT TO SCALE

DECK

Plate No. 1

PADEYE (3) Detail "B"

BOTTOM

(WINCH)

MOUSETRAP (REF.) (DOWN POSIT.)

DRAWN BY Robert K. Baldwin

SIDE

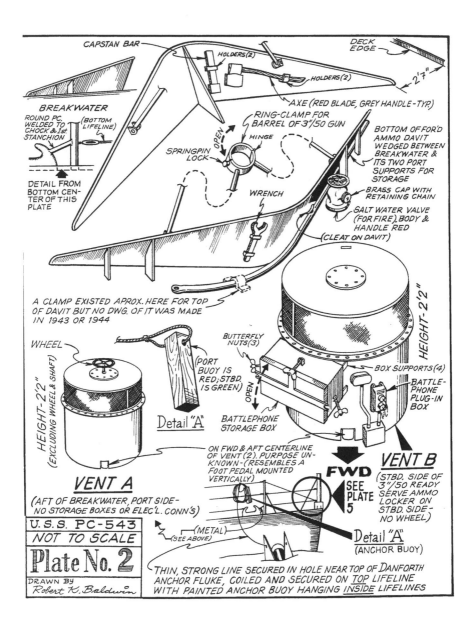

CAPSTAN BAR

HOLDERS (2)

DECK EDGE

HOLDERS (2)

2'7"

BREAKWATER

ROUND PC. WELDED TO CHOCK & 1st STANCHION

(BOTTOM LIFELINE)

AXE (RED BLADE, GREY HANDLE - TYP.)

RING-CLAMP FOR BARREL OF 3"/50 GUN

OPEN

HINGE

SPRINGPIN LOCK

BOTTOM OF FOR'D AMMO DAVIT WEDGED BETWEEN BREAKWATER & ITS TWO PORT SUPPORTS FOR STORAGE

BRASS CAP WITH RETAINING CHAIN

WRENCH

SALT WATER VALVE (FOR FIRE), BODY & HANDLE RED

DETAIL FROM BOTTOM CENTER OF THIS PLATE

(CLEAT ON DAVIT)

HEIGHT - 2'2"

A CLAMP EXISTED APROX. HERE FOR TOP OF DAVIT BUT NO DWG. OF IT WAS MADE IN 1943 OR 1944

WHEEL

BUTTERFLY NUTS (3)

(PORT BUOY IS RED; STBD. IS GREEN)

BOX SUPPORTS (4)

BATTLE-PHONE PLUG-IN BOX

HEIGHT - 2'2" (EXCLUDING WHEEL & SHAFT)

Detail "A"

OPEN

BATTLEPHONE STORAGE BOX

Detail "A"

ON FWD & AFT CENTERLINE OF VENT (2). PURPOSE UN-KNOWN - (RESEMBLES A FOOT PEDAL MOUNTED VERTICALLY)

FWD
SEE
PLATE
5

VENT B

(STBD. SIDE OF 3"/50 READY SERVE AMMO LOCKER ON STBD. SIDE - NO WHEEL)

VENT A

(AFT OF BREAKWATER, PORT SIDE - NO STORAGE BOXES OR ELEC'L. CONN'S)

U.S.S. PC-543
NOT TO SCALE
Plate No. 2
DRAWN BY
Robert K. Baldwin

(METAL) (SEE ABOVE)

Detail "A"
(ANCHOR BUOY)

THIN, STRONG LINE SECURED IN HOLE NEAR TOP OF DANFORTH ANCHOR FLUKE, COILED AND SECURED ON TOP LIFELINE WITH PAINTED ANCHOR BUOY HANGING INSIDE LIFELINES

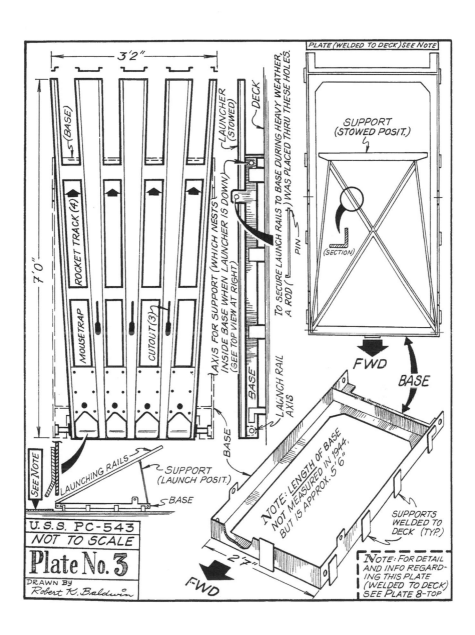

3'2"

(BASE)

ROCKET TRACK (4)

MOUSETRAP

CUTOUT (3)

7'0"

LAUNCHER (STOWED)

DECK

BASE

BASE

LAUNCH RAIL AXIS

AXIS FOR SUPPORT (WHICH NESTS INSIDE BASE WHEN LAUNCHER IS DOWN) (SEE TOP VIEW AT RIGHT)

TO SECURE LAUNCH RAILS TO BASE DURING HEAVY WEATHER, A ROD (——PIN ——➤) WAS PLACED THRU THESE HOLES.

PLATE (WELDED TO DECK) SEE NOTE

SUPPORT (STOWED POSIT.)

(SECTION)

FWD

BASE

SEE NOTE

LAUNCHING RAILS

SUPPORT (LAUNCH POSIT.)

BASE

NOTE: LENGTH OF BASE NOT MEASURED IN 1944, BUT IS APPROX. 5'6"

SUPPORTS WELDED TO DECK (TYP.)

U.S.S. PC-543

NOT TO SCALE

Plate No. 3

DRAWN BY
Robert K. Baldwin

2'7"

FWD

NOTE: FOR DETAIL AND INFO REGARD-ING THIS PLATE (WELDED TO DECK) SEE PLATE 8-TOP

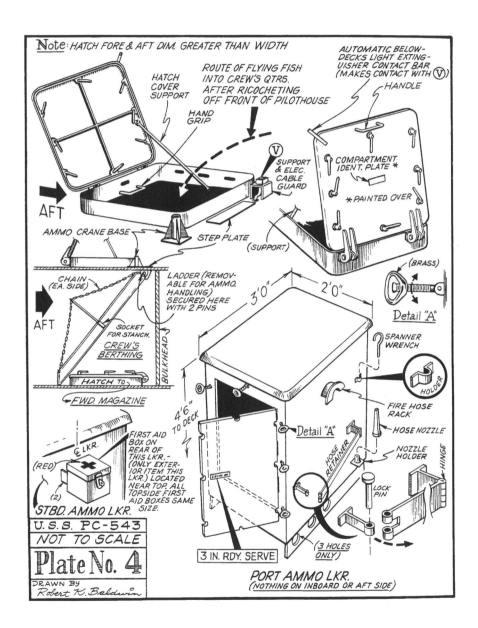

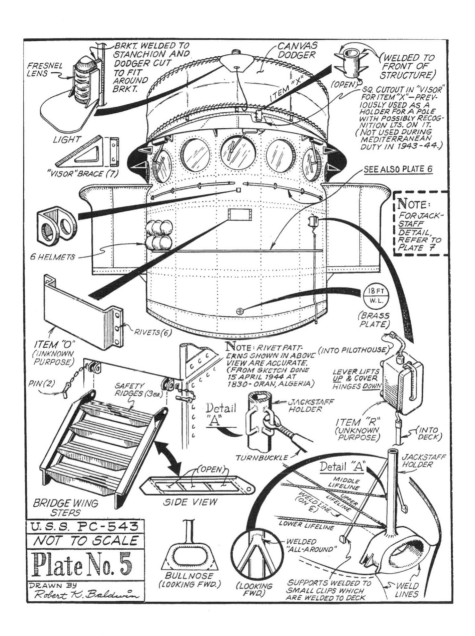

FRESNEL LENS

BRKT. WELDED TO STANCHION AND DODGER CUT TO FIT AROUND BRKT.

CANVAS DODGER

ITEM "X"

(OPEN)

(WELDED TO FRONT OF STRUCTURE)

SQ. CUTOUT IN "VISOR" FOR ITEM "X"—PREVIOUSLY USED AS A HOLDER FOR A POLE WITH POSSIBLY RECOGNITION LTS. ON IT. (NOT USED DURING MEDITERRANEAN DUTY IN 1943-44.)

LIGHT

"VISOR" BRACE (7)

SEE ALSO PLATE 6

NOTE: FOR JACK-STAFF DETAIL, REFER TO PLATE 7

6 HELMETS

18 FT W.L.

(BRASS PLATE)

ITEM "O" (UNKNOWN PURPOSE)

RIVETS (6)

NOTE: RIVET PATTERNS SHOWN IN ABOVE VIEW ARE ACCURATE. (FROM SKETCH DONE 15 APRIL 1944 AT 1830 - ORAN, ALGERIA)

(INTO PILOTHOUSE)

LEVER LIFTS UP & COVER HINGES DOWN

PIN (2)

SAFETY RIDGES (3 ea.)

Detail "A"

JACKSTAFF HOLDER

ITEM "R" (UNKNOWN PURPOSE)

(INTO DECK)

JACKSTAFF HOLDER

TURNBUCKLE

Detail "A"

MIDDLE LIFELINE

UPPER LIFELINE

WELD LINE (ON ℄)

LOWER LIFELINE

BRIDGE WING STEPS

(OPEN)

SIDE VIEW

U.S.S. PC-543

NOT TO SCALE

Plate No. 5

DRAWN BY Robert K. Baldwin

BULLNOSE (LOOKING FWD.)

(LOOKING FWD.)

WELDED "ALL-AROUND"

SUPPORTS WELDED TO SMALL CLIPS WHICH ARE WELDED TO DECK

WELD LINES

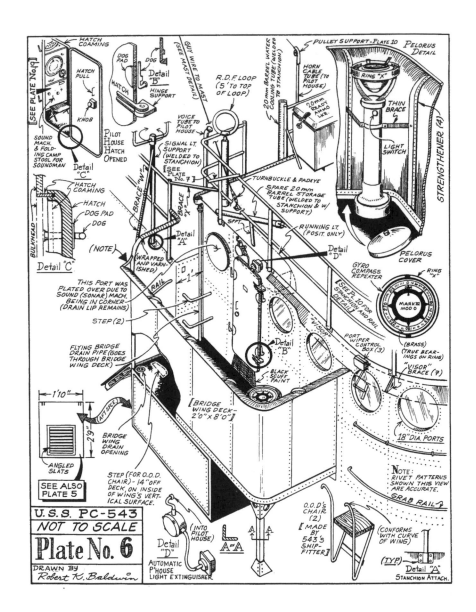

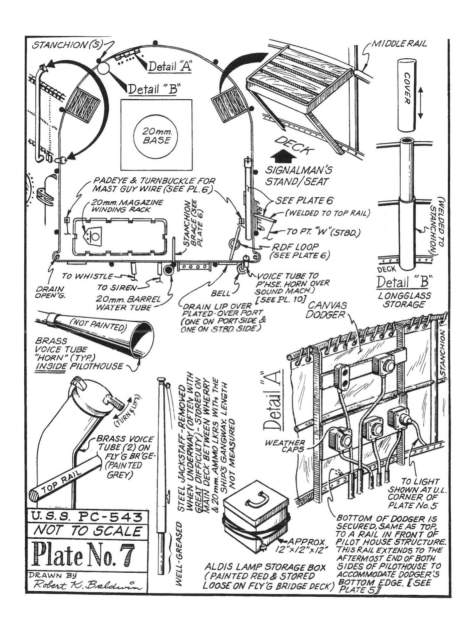

STANCHION (S)

Detail "A"

Detail "B"

MIDDLE RAIL

COVER

20mm. BASE

DECK

SIGNALMAN'S STAND/SEAT

SEE PLATE 6
(WELDED TO TOP RAIL)

TO PT. "W" (STBD.)

RDF LOOP
(SEE PLATE 6)

(WELDED TO STANCHION)

DECK

Detail "B"
LONGGLASS STORAGE

PADEYE & TURNBUCKLE FOR MAST GUY WIRE (SEE PL. 6)

20mm. MAGAZINE WINDING RACK

STANCHION BRACE (SEE PLATE 6)

TO WHISTLE

DRAIN OPEN'G.

TO SIREN

20mm. BARREL WATER TUBE

BELL

DRAIN LIP OVER PLATED-OVER PORT (ONE ON PORT SIDE & ONE ON STBD. SIDE)

VOICE TUBE TO P'HSE. HORN OVER SOUND MACH.)
[SEE PL. 10]

(NOT PAINTED)

BRASS VOICE TUBE "HORN" (TYP.) INSIDE PILOTHOUSE

CANVAS DODGER

Detail "A"

WEATHER CAPS

STANCHION

(TURN & LIFT)

BRASS VOICE TUBE (2) ON FLY'G BR'GE (PAINTED GREY)

TOP RAIL

STEEL JACKSTAFF-REMOVED WHEN UNDERWAY (OFTEN WITH GREAT DIFFICULTY)-STORED ON MAIN DECK BETWEEN WHERRY & 20mm. AMMO LKRS WITH THE SHIP'S GANGWAY. LENGTH NOT MEASURED

TO LIGHT SHOWN AT U.L. CORNER OF PLATE No. 5

U.S.S. PC-543
NOT TO SCALE
Plate No. 7
DRAWN BY
Robert K. Baldwin

WELL-GREASED

APPROX. 12"x12"x12"

ALDIS LAMP STORAGE BOX
(PAINTED RED & STORED LOOSE ON FLY'G BRIDGE DECK)

BOTTOM OF DODGER IS SECURED, SAME AS TOP, TO A RAIL IN FRONT OF PILOT HOUSE STRUCTURE. THIS RAIL EXTENDS TO THE AFTERMOST END OF BOTH SIDES OF PILOTHOUSE TO ACCOMMODATE DODGER'S BOTTOM EDGE. [SEE PLATE 5]

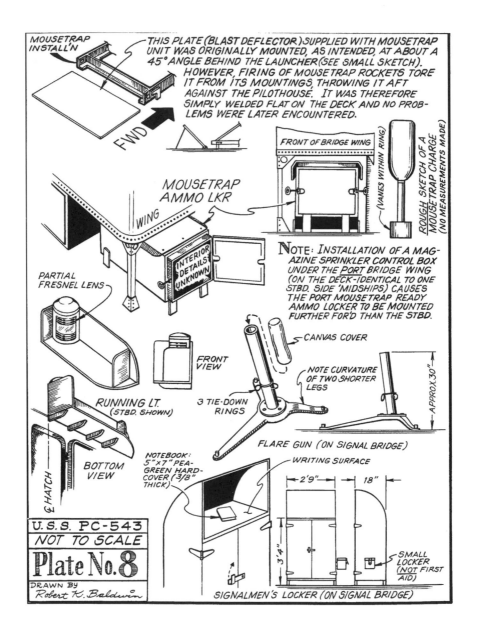

MOUSETRAP INSTALL'N

THIS PLATE (BLAST DEFLECTOR) SUPPLIED WITH MOUSETRAP UNIT WAS ORIGINALLY MOUNTED, AS INTENDED, AT ABOUT A 45° ANGLE BEHIND THE LAUNCHER (SEE SMALL SKETCH). HOWEVER, FIRING OF MOUSETRAP ROCKETS TORE IT FROM ITS MOUNTINGS, THROWING IT AFT AGAINST THE PILOTHOUSE. IT WAS THEREFORE SIMPLY WELDED FLAT ON THE DECK AND NO PROBLEMS WERE LATER ENCOUNTERED.

FWD

FRONT OF BRIDGE WING

(VANES WITHIN RING)

ROUGH SKETCH OF A MOUSETRAP CHARGE (NO MEASUREMENTS MADE)

MOUSETRAP AMMO LKR

WING

INTERIOR DETAILS UNKNOWN

NOTE: INSTALLATION OF A MAGAZINE SPRINKLER CONTROL BOX UNDER THE PORT BRIDGE WING (ON THE DECK-IDENTICAL TO ONE STBD. SIDE 'MIDSHIPS) CAUSES THE PORT MOUSETRAP READY AMMO LOCKER TO BE MOUNTED FURTHER FOR'D THAN THE STBD.

PARTIAL FRESNEL LENS

FRONT VIEW

CANVAS COVER

NOTE CURVATURE OF TWO SHORTER LEGS

APPROX. 30"

RUNNING LT. (STBD. SHOWN)

3 TIE-DOWN RINGS

FLARE GUN (ON SIGNAL BRIDGE)

℄ HATCH

BOTTOM VIEW

NOTEBOOK: 5"x7" PEA-GREEN HARD-COVER (3/8" THICK)

WRITING SURFACE

U.S.S. PC-543
NOT TO SCALE
Plate No. 8
DRAWN BY
Robert K. Baldwin

2'9"   18"

3'4"

SMALL LOCKER (NOT FIRST AID)

SIGNALMEN'S LOCKER (ON SIGNAL BRIDGE)

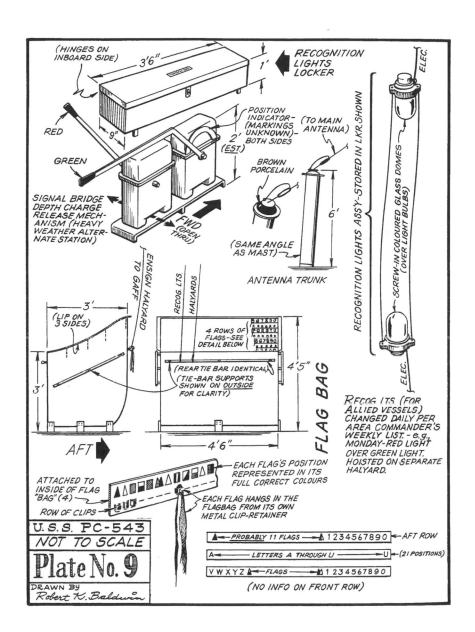

(HINGES ON INBOARD SIDE)

3'6"

1'

RECOGNITION LIGHTS LOCKER

RED

9"

GREEN

POSITION INDICATOR – (MARKINGS UNKNOWN) – BOTH SIDES

(TO MAIN ANTENNA)

2' (EST.)

BROWN PORCELAIN

SIGNAL BRIDGE DEPTH CHARGE RELEASE MECHANISM (HEAVY WEATHER ALTERNATE STATION)

FWD (OPEN THRU)

(SAME ANGLE AS MAST)

ANTENNA TRUNK

RECOGNITION LIGHTS ASS'Y – STORED IN LKR. SHOWN

ELEC.

SCREW-IN COLOURED GLASS DOMES (OVER LIGHT BULBS)

6'

ELEC.

ENSIGN HALYARD TO GAFF

RECOG. LTS. HALYARDS

3'

(LIP ON 3 SIDES)

3'

4 ROWS OF FLAGS – SEE DETAIL BELOW

(REAR TIE BAR IDENTICAL)
(TIE-BAR SUPPORTS SHOWN ON OUTSIDE FOR CLARITY)

4'5"

FLAG BAG

AFT

4'6"

RECOG. LTS. (FOR ALLIED VESSELS) CHANGED DAILY PER AREA COMMANDER'S WEEKLY LIST – e.g., MONDAY-RED LIGHT OVER GREEN LIGHT. HOISTED ON SEPARATE HALYARD.

EACH FLAG'S POSITION REPRESENTED IN ITS FULL CORRECT COLOURS

ATTACHED TO INSIDE OF FLAG "BAG" (4)

ROW OF CLIPS

EACH FLAG HANGS IN THE FLAGBAG FROM ITS OWN METAL CLIP-RETAINER

U.S.S. PC-543
NOT TO SCALE
Plate No. 9
DRAWN BY
Robert K. Baldwin

◄— PROBABLY 11 FLAGS —► 1234567890 ◄AFT ROW

A ◄— LETTERS A THROUGH U —► U ◄(21 POSITIONS)

V W X Y Z ◄—FLAGS—► 1234567890

(NO INFO ON FRONT ROW)

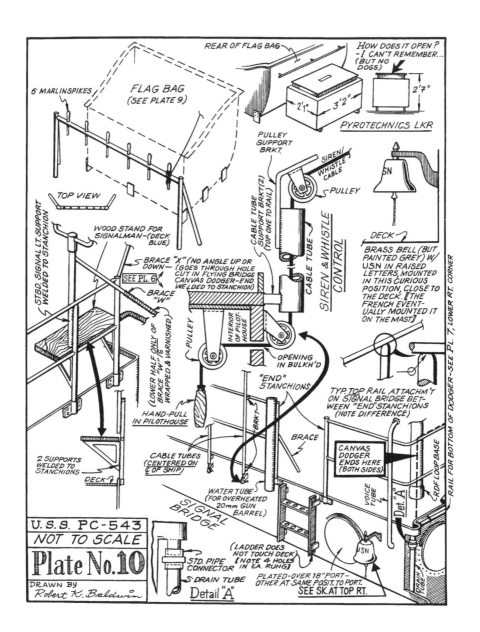

REAR OF FLAG BAG

HOW DOES IT OPEN? – I CAN'T REMEMBER... (BUT NO DOGS)

FLAG BAG (SEE PLATE 9)

6 MARLINSPIKES

2'7"

2'1" — 3'2"

PYROTECHNICS LKR

PULLEY SUPPORT BRKT.

SIREN/WHISTLE CABLE

PULLEY

SN

TOP VIEW

CABLE TUBE SUPPORT BRKT (2) (TOP ONE TO RAIL)

DECK

BRASS BELL (BUT PAINTED GREY) W/ USN IN RAISED LETTERS, MOUNTED IN THIS CURIOUS POSITION, CLOSE TO THE DECK. [THE FRENCH EVENTUALLY MOUNTED IT ON THE MAST]

STBD. SIGNAL LT. SUPPORT WELDED TO STANCHION

WOOD STAND FOR SIGNALMAN–(DECK BLUE)

BRACE "X" (NO ANGLE UP OR DOWN— (GOES THROUGH HOLE CUT IN FLYING BRIDGE CANVAS DODGER–END WELDED TO STANCHION)

SEE PL. 6

BRACE "W"

SIREN & WHISTLE CONTROL

CABLE TUBE

(LOWER HALF ONLY OF BRACE "W" IS WRAPPED & VARNISHED)

PULLEY

INTERIOR OF PILOT HOUSE

OPENING IN BULKH'D

HAND-PULL IN PILOTHOUSE

"END" STANCHIONS

TYP. TOP RAIL ATTACHM'T ON SIGNAL BRIDGE BETWEEN "END" STANCHIONS (NOTE DIFFERENCE)

RAIL FOR BOTTOM OF DODGER–SEE PL. 7, LOWER RT. CORNER

2 SUPPORTS WELDED TO STANCHIONS

DECK

BRKT

BRACE

CANVAS DODGER ENDS HERE (BOTH SIDES)

RDF LOOP BASE

CABLE TUBES (CENTERED ON ₵ OF SHIP)

WATER TUBE (FOR OVERHEATED 20mm GUN BARREL)

VOICE TUBE

Det. "A"

SIGNAL BRIDGE

U.S.S. PC-543

NOT TO SCALE

Plate No. 10

DRAWN BY Robert K. Baldwin

STD. PIPE CONNECTOR

DRAIN TUBE

Detail "A"

(LADDER DOES NOT TOUCH DECK) [NOTE 4 HOLES IN EA. RUNG]

SN

PLATED-OVER 18" PORT– OTHER AT SAME POSIT. TO PORT. SEE SK. AT TOP RT.

DRAIN TUBE

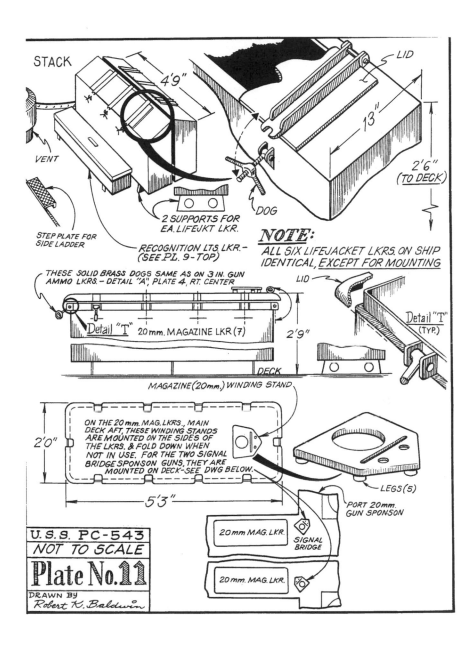

STACK

4'9"

LID

13"

VENT

2'6"
(TO DECK)

STEP PLATE FOR
SIDE LADDER

2 SUPPORTS FOR
EA. LIFEJKT. LKR.

DOG

RECOGNITION LTS. LKR.—
(SEE PL. 9—TOP)

NOTE:

ALL SIX LIFEJACKET LKRS. ON SHIP
IDENTICAL, *EXCEPT FOR MOUNTING*

THESE SOLID BRASS DOGS SAME AS ON 3 IN. GUN
AMMO LKRS.— DETAIL "A", PLATE 4, RT. CENTER

LID

Detail "T" 20 mm. MAGAZINE LKR (7)

2'9"

Detail "T"
(TYP.)

DECK

MAGAZINE (20mm.) WINDING STAND

2'0"

ON THE 20 mm. MAG. LKRS., MAIN
DECK AFT, THESE WINDING STANDS
ARE MOUNTED ON THE SIDES OF
THE LKRS. & FOLD DOWN WHEN
NOT IN USE. FOR THE TWO SIGNAL
BRIDGE SPONSON GUNS, THEY ARE
MOUNTED ON DECK—SEE DWG BELOW.

LEGS(5)

PORT 20mm.
GUN SPONSON

5'3"

20 mm. MAG. LKR.

SIGNAL
BRIDGE

U.S.S. PC-543
NOT TO SCALE
Plate No. 11
DRAWN BY
Robert K. Baldwin

20 mm. MAG. LKR.

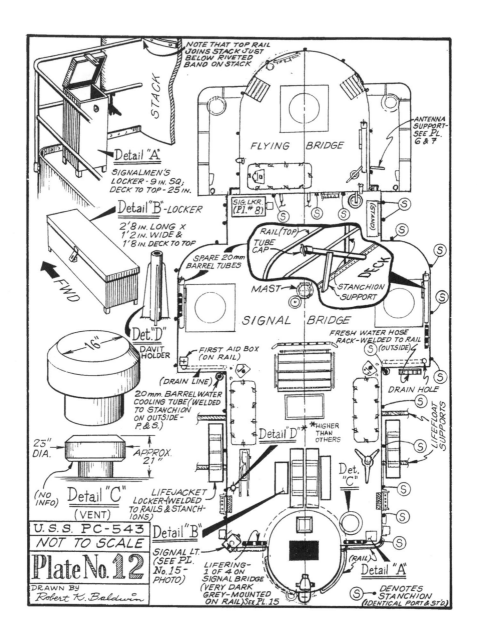

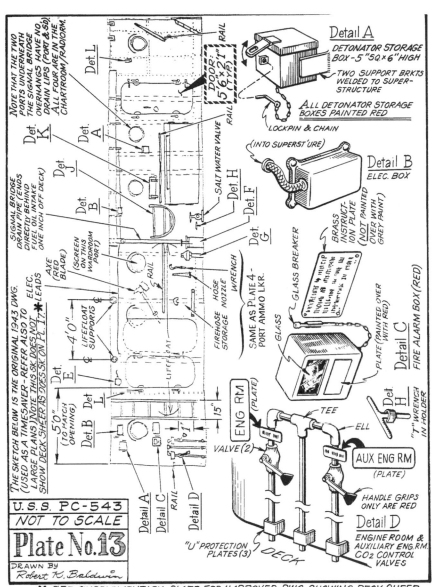

Detail A
DETONATOR STORAGE
BOX – 5"SQ. × 6" HIGH
TWO SUPPORT BRKTS
WELDED TO SUPER-
STRUCTURE
ALL DETONATOR STORAGE
BOXES PAINTED RED
LOCKPIN & CHAIN

(INTO SUPERST'URE)
Detail B
ELEC. BOX

BRASS INSTRUCT-
ION PLATE
(NOT PAINTED
OVER WITH
GREY PAINT)

GLASS BREAKER

GLASS

PLATE (PAINTED OVER
WITH RED)

Detail C
FIRE ALARM BOX (RED)

DOOR – 5'6" × 2'1"
(TYP.)

SALT WATER VALVE

Det. L

Det. K

Det. A

Det. J

Det. B

Det. E

Det. B

Det. B

Det. L

Det. H

Det. F

Det. G

Det. H
"T" WRENCH
IN HOLDER

NOTE THAT THE TWO PORTS UNDERNEATH THE SIGNAL BRIDGE OVERHANGS HAVE NO DRAIN LIPS (PORT & Sd). ALL FOUR ARE IN THE CHARTROOM/RADIO RM.

SIGNAL BRIDGE DRAIN PIPE (ENDS DIRECTLY BEHIND FUEL OIL INTAKE ONE INCH OFF DECK)

ELEC.
LEADS

AXE
(RED
BLADE)

(SCREEN
ON THIS
WARDROOM
PORT)

RAIL

HOSE
NOZZLE

WRENCH

FIREHOSE
STORAGE

SAME AS PLATE 4 -
PORT AMMO LKR.

LIFEFLOAT
SUPPORTS

4'-0"

15"

5'-0"
(TO HATCH
OPENING)

THE SKETCH BELOW IS THE ORIGINAL 1943 DWG. (USED AS A TIMESAVER – REFER ALSO TO LARGE PLANS) NOTE THIS SK DOES NOT SHOW DECK SHEER AS DOES SK ON PL. 17.

ENG RM
(PLATE)

TEE

ELL

VALVE (2)

AUX ENG RM
(PLATE)

HANDLE GRIPS
ONLY ARE RED

Detail D
ENGINE ROOM &
AUXILIARY ENG. RM.
CO2 CONTROL
VALVES

"U" PROTECTION
PLATES (3)

DECK

Detail A

Detail C

Detail D

RAIL

U.S.S. PC-543
NOT TO SCALE
Plate No. 13
DRAWN BY
Robert K. Baldwin

★ SEE SUPPLEMENTARY PLATE FOR IMPROVED DWG. SHOWING DECK SHEER

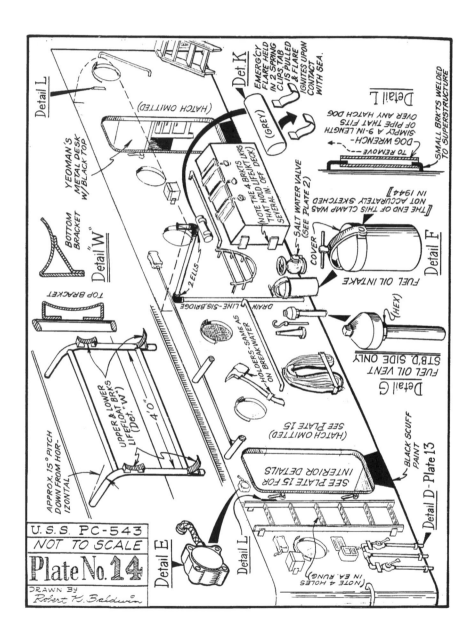

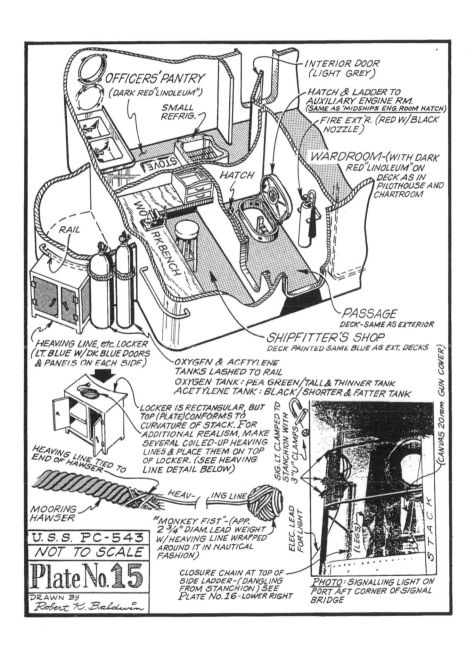

OFFICERS' PANTRY
(DARK RED "LINOLEUM")

INTERIOR DOOR
(LIGHT GREY)

HATCH & LADDER TO
AUXILIARY ENGINE RM.
(SAME AS 'MIDSHIPS ENG. ROOM HATCH)

SMALL
REFRIG.

FIRE EXT'R. (RED W/BLACK
NOZZLE)

STOVE

HATCH

WARDROOM-(WITH DARK
RED "LINOLEUM" ON
DECK AS IN
PILOTHOUSE AND
CHARTROOM

RAIL

WORKBENCH

PASSAGE
DECK-SAME AS EXTERIOR

SHIPFITTER'S SHOP
DECK PAINTED SAME BLUE AS EXT. DECKS

HEAVING LINE, etc. LOCKER
(LT. BLUE W/DK. BLUE DOORS
& PANELS ON EACH SIDE)

OXYGEN & ACETYLENE
TANKS LASHED TO RAIL
OXYGEN TANK: PEA GREEN/TALL & THINNER TANK
ACETYLENE TANK: BLACK/SHORTER & FATTER TANK

LOCKER IS RECTANGULAR, BUT
TOP (PLATE) CONFORMS TO
CURVATURE OF STACK. FOR
ADDITIONAL REALISM, MAKE
SEVERAL COILED-UP HEAVING
LINES & PLACE THEM ON TOP
OF LOCKER. (SEE HEAVING
LINE DETAIL BELOW)

SIG. LT. CLAMPED TO
STANCHION WITH
3 "U" CLAMPS

(CANVAS 20mm GUN COVER)

HEAVING LINE TIED TO
END OF HAWSER

HEAV-   ING LINE

MOORING
HAWSER

ELEC. LEAD
FOR LIGHT

(LEGS)

STACK

U.S.S. PC-543
NOT TO SCALE
Plate No. 15
DRAWN BY
Robert K. Baldwin

"MONKEY FIST"- (APP.
2 3/4" DIAM. LEAD WEIGHT
W/ HEAVING LINE WRAPPED
AROUND IT IN NAUTICAL
FASHION)

CLOSURE CHAIN AT TOP OF
SIDE LADDER - (DANGLING
FROM STANCHION) SEE
PLATE No. 16 - LOWER RIGHT

PHOTO: SIGNALLING LIGHT ON
PORT AFT CORNER OF SIGNAL
BRIDGE

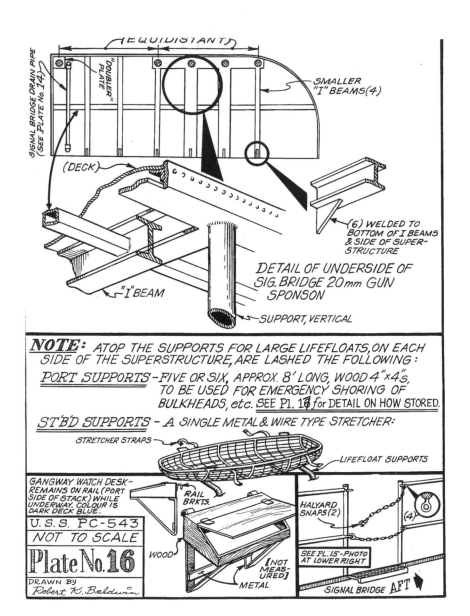

(EQUIDISTANT)

SIGNAL BRIDGE DRAIN PIPE
(SEE PLATE No. 14)

"DOUBLER"
PLATE

SMALLER
"I" BEAMS (4)

(DECK)

(6) WELDED TO
BOTTOM OF I BEAMS
& SIDE OF SUPER-
STRUCTURE

"I" BEAM

DETAIL OF UNDERSIDE OF
SIG. BRIDGE 20mm GUN
SPONSON

SUPPORT, VERTICAL

NOTE: *ATOP THE SUPPORTS FOR LARGE LIFEFLOATS, ON EACH
SIDE OF THE SUPERSTRUCTURE, ARE LASHED THE FOLLOWING:*

<u>PORT SUPPORTS</u> *–FIVE OR SIX, APPROX. 8' LONG, WOOD 4"x4's,
TO BE USED FOR EMERGENCY SHORING OF
BULKHEADS, etc.* SEE Pl. 16 *for DETAIL ON HOW STORED.*

<u>ST'B'D SUPPORTS</u> *– A SINGLE METAL & WIRE TYPE STRETCHER:*

STRETCHER STRAPS

LIFEFLOAT SUPPORTS

GANGWAY WATCH DESK-
REMAINS ON RAIL (PORT
SIDE OF STACK) WHILE
UNDERWAY. COLOUR IS
DARK DECK BLUE.

RAIL
BRKTS.

HALYARD
SNAPS (2)

(4)

U.S.S. PC-543

NOT TO SCALE

Plate No. 16

DRAWN BY
Robert K. Baldwin

WOOD

[NOT
MEAS-
URED]

METAL

SEE PL. 15-PHOTO
AT LOWER RIGHT

SIGNAL BRIDGE AFT

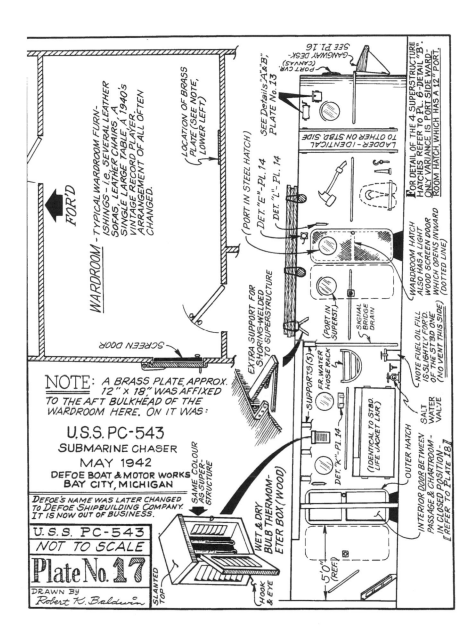

FOR'D

WARDROOM - TYPICAL WARDROOM FURN-ISHINGS - i.e., SEVERAL LEATHER SOFAS, LEATHER CHAIRS, A SINGLE LARGE TABLE, A 1940's VINTAGE RECORD PLAYER. ARRANGEMENT OF ALL OFTEN CHANGED.

(LOCATION OF BRASS PLATE (SEE NOTE, LOWER LEFT)

SCREEN DOOR

NOTE: A BRASS PLATE, APPROX. 12" X 18" WAS AFFIXED TO THE AFT BULKHEAD OF THE WARDROOM HERE. ON IT WAS:

U.S.S. PC-543
SUBMARINE CHASER
MAY 1942
DEFOE BOAT & MOTOR WORKS
BAY CITY, MICHIGAN

DEFOE'S NAME WAS LATER CHANGED TO DEFOE SHIPBUILDING COMPANY. IT IS NOW OUT OF BUSINESS.

U.S.S. PC-543
NOT TO SCALE
Plate No. 17
DRAWN BY
Robert K. Baldwin

SAME COLOUR AS SUPER-STRUCTURE

WET & DRY BULB THERMOM-ETER BOX (WOOD)

SLANTED TOP

HOOK & EYE

EXTRA SUPPORT FOR SHORING-WELDED TO SUPERSTRUCTURE

(PORT IN STEEL HATCH)

DET. "E"- PL. 14

DET. "L"- PL. 14

(PORT IN SUPERST.)

SIGNAL BRIDGE DRAIN

WARDROOM HATCH ALSO HAS A LIGHT WOOD SCREEN DOOR WHICH OPENS INWARD (DOTTED LINE)

SUPPORTS (5)

FR. WATER HOSE RACK

DET "K"- PL. 14

(IDENTICAL TO STBD LIFE JACKET LKR.)

OUTER HATCH

NOTE FUEL OIL FILL IS SLIGHTLY FOR'D. OF THE ST'BD ONE (NO VENT THIS SIDE)

SALT WATER VALVE

INTERIOR DOOR BETWEEN PASSAGE & CHARTROOM - IN CLOSED POSITION - REFER TO PLATE 18.

5'0" (REF.)

PORT CVR. (CANVAS) (GANGWAY DESK-SEE PL.16.

SEE Details "A"& "B", PLATE No. 13

LADDER - IDENTICAL TO OTHER ON STB'D. SIDE

FOR DETAIL OF THE 4 SUPERSTRUCTURE HATCHES REFER TO PL. 6-DETAIL "B". ONLY VARIANCE IS PORT SIDE WARD-ROOM HATCH WHICH HAS A 12" PORT.

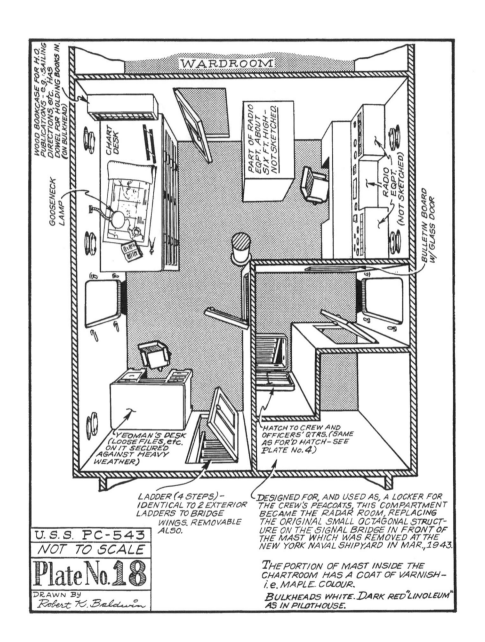

WARDROOM

WOOD BOOKCASE FOR H.O. PUBLICATIONS - e.g.: SAILING DIRECTIONS, etc. HAS DOWEL FOR HOLDING BOOKS IN. (ON BULKHEAD)

CHART DESK

GOOSENECK LAMP

PART OF RADIO EQPT. ABOUT SIX FT. HIGH - NOT SKETCHED

RADIO EQPT. (NOT SKETCHED)

BULLETIN BOARD W/ GLASS DOOR

YEOMAN'S DESK (LOOSE FILES, etc. ON IT SECURED AGAINST HEAVY WEATHER)

HATCH TO CREW AND OFFICERS' QTRS. (SAME AS FOR'D HATCH- SEE PLATE No. 4)

LADDER (4 STEPS) - IDENTICAL TO 2 EXTERIOR LADDERS TO BRIDGE WINGS. REMOVABLE ALSO.

DESIGNED FOR, AND USED AS, A LOCKER FOR THE CREW'S PEACOATS, THIS COMPARTMENT BECAME THE RADAR ROOM, REPLACING THE ORIGINAL SMALL OCTAGONAL STRUCT-URE ON THE SIGNAL BRIDGE IN FRONT OF THE MAST WHICH WAS REMOVED AT THE NEW YORK NAVAL SHIPYARD IN MAR., 1943.

THE PORTION OF MAST INSIDE THE CHARTROOM HAS A COAT OF VARNISH- i.e. MAPLE COLOUR.

BULKHEADS WHITE. DARK RED "LINOLEUM" AS IN PILOTHOUSE.

U.S.S. PC-543
NOT TO SCALE
Plate No. 18
DRAWN BY
Robert K. Baldwin

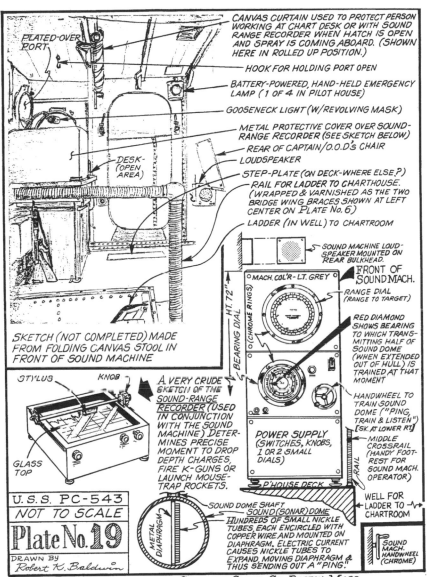

CANVAS CURTAIN USED TO PROTECT PERSON
WORKING AT CHART DESK OR WITH SOUND
RANGE RECORDER WHEN HATCH IS OPEN
AND SPRAY IS COMING ABOARD. (SHOWN
HERE IN ROLLED UP POSITION.)

PLATED-OVER PORT

HOOK FOR HOLDING PORT OPEN

BATTERY-POWERED, HAND-HELD EMERGENCY
LAMP (1 OF 4 IN PILOT HOUSE)

GOOSENECK LIGHT (W/REVOLVING MASK)

METAL PROTECTIVE COVER OVER SOUND-
RANGE RECORDER (SEE SKETCH BELOW)

REAR OF CAPTAIN/O.O.D's CHAIR

DESK (OPEN AREA)

LOUDSPEAKER

STEP-PLATE (ON DECK-WHERE ELSE?)

RAIL FOR LADDER TO CHARTHOUSE.
(WRAPPED & VARNISHED AS THE TWO
BRIDGE WING BRACES SHOWN AT LEFT
CENTER ON PLATE No. 6)

LADDER (IN WELL) TO CHARTROOM

SOUND MACHINE LOUD-
SPEAKER MOUNTED ON
REAR BULKHEAD.

FRONT OF SOUND MACH.

MACH. COL'R - LT. GREY

RANGE DIAL
(RANGE TO TARGET)

RED DIAMOND
SHOWS BEARING
TO WHICH TRANS-
MITTING HALF OF
SOUND DOME
(WHEN EXTENDED
OUT OF HULL) IS
TRAINED AT THAT
MOMENT

SKETCH (NOT COMPLETED) MADE
FROM FOLDING CANVAS STOOL IN
FRONT OF SOUND MACHINE

HT. 72"

BEARING DIAL

(CHROME RINGS)

STYLUS   KNOB

A VERY CRUDE
SKETCH OF THE
SOUND-RANGE
RECORDER (USED
IN CONJUNCTION
WITH THE SOUND
MACHINE) DETER-
MINES PRECISE
MOMENT TO DROP
DEPTH CHARGES,
FIRE K-GUNS OR
LAUNCH MOUSE-
TRAP ROCKETS.

GLASS TOP

POWER SUPPLY
(SWITCHES, KNOBS,
1 OR 2 SMALL
DIALS)

HANDWHEEL TO
TRAIN SOUND
DOME ("PING,
TRAIN & LISTEN")
[SK. AT LOWER RT]

MIDDLE
CROSSRAIL
(HANDY FOOT-
REST FOR
SOUND MACH.
OPERATOR)

RAIL

P'HOUSE DECK

WELL FOR
LADDER TO
CHARTROOM

U.S.S. PC-543
NOT TO SCALE

Plate No. 19

DRAWN BY
Robert K. Baldwin

SOUND DOME SHAFT

SOUND (SONAR) DOME
HUNDREDS OF SMALL NICKLE
TUBES, EACH ENCIRCLED WITH
COPPER WIRE AND MOUNTED ON
DIAPHRAGM. ELECTRIC CURRENT
CAUSES NICKLE TUBES TO
EXPAND, MOVING DIAPHRAGM &
THUS SENDING OUT A "PING."

METAL DIAPHRAGM

SOUND MACH. HANDWHEEL (CHROME)

MF'R. OF SOUND MACH. & RECORDER: SUBMARINE SIGNAL CO., BOSTON, MASS.

Although not pertinent to building a model, you will probably be interested in knowing that the hulls of many, if not all, of these submarine chasers were built upside down to speed their production.

Since there is far more welding on any overhead compared to the amount of welding on a deck (which must, of course, be kept as unobstructed as possible for walking) building hulls upside down allows welders to work at their feet rather than over their heads, a far easier and faster operation.

Many PC boats built along rivers were launched down ways <u>sideways</u> since some river construction sites did not have the room for conventional launching. Thus, the hull of a PC was started on one set of ways and then was "rolled over" to adjoining ways (see sketches at bottom, this page). The prefabricated super-structure was then lowered by cranes onto the hull.

The boxed sketch at lower left is based solely on recollec-tions of a comprehensive magazine article (since lost) showing the construction of PCs at Defoe Boat and Motor Works - later Defoe Shipbuilding Company, but now out of business.

This article was illustrated with a number of fine photo-graphs and appeared in either a January or February issue of YACHTING magazine in 1942. The sketches are, therefore, far from accurate as to details.

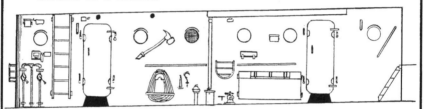

IMPROVED SK. OF SUPERSTRUCTURE (STBD. SIDE) FROM THAT ON PLATE 13 SHOWING A TRUE VIEW WITH MAIN DECK SHEER

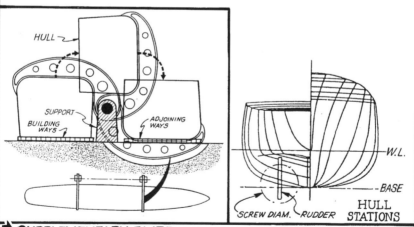

▶ SUPPLEMENTARY PLATE

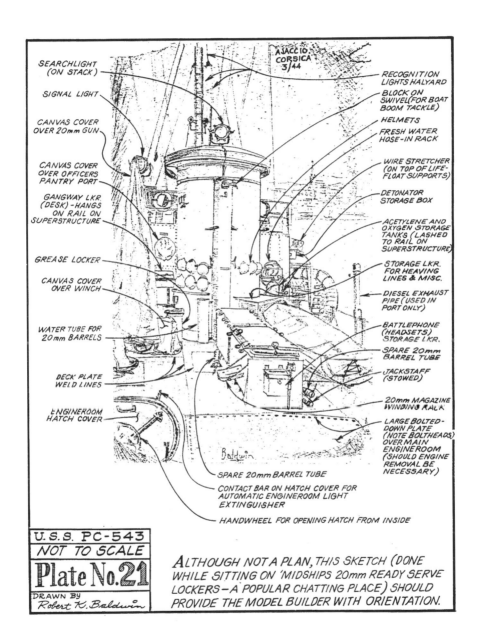

AJACCIO
CORSICA
3/44

SEARCHLIGHT
(ON STACK)

SIGNAL LIGHT

CANVAS COVER
OVER 20mm GUN

CANVAS COVER
OVER OFFICERS
PANTRY PORT

GANGWAY LKR.
(DESK)—HANGS
ON RAIL ON
SUPERSTRUCTURE

GREASE LOCKER

CANVAS COVER
OVER WINCH

WATER TUBE FOR
20mm BARRELS

DECK PLATE
WELD LINES

ENGINEROOM
HATCH COVER

RECOGNITION
LIGHTS HALYARD

BLOCK ON
SWIVEL(FOR BOAT
BOOM TACKLE)

HELMETS

FRESH WATER
HOSE-IN RACK

WIRE STRETCHER
(ON TOP OF LIFE-
FLOAT SUPPORTS)

DETONATOR
STORAGE BOX

ACETYLENE AND
OXYGEN STORAGE
TANKS (LASHED
TO RAIL ON
SUPERSTRUCTURE)

STORAGE LKR.
FOR HEAVING
LINES & MISC.

DIESEL EXHAUST
PIPE (USED IN
PORT ONLY)

BATTLEPHONE
(HEADSETS)
STORAGE LKR.

SPARE 20mm
BARREL TUBE

JACKSTAFF
(STOWED)

20mm MAGAZINE
WINDING RACK

LARGE BOLTED-
DOWN PLATE
(NOTE BOLTHEADS)
OVER MAIN
ENGINEROOM
(SHOULD ENGINE
REMOVAL BE
NECESSARY)

Baldwin

SPARE 20mm BARREL TUBE

CONTACT BAR ON HATCH COVER FOR
AUTOMATIC ENGINEROOM LIGHT
EXTINGUISHER

HANDWHEEL FOR OPENING HATCH FROM INSIDE

U.S.S. PC-543
NOT TO SCALE
Plate No.21
DRAWN BY
Robert K. Baldwin

ALTHOUGH NOT A PLAN, THIS SKETCH (DONE
WHILE SITTING ON 'MIDSHIPS 20mm READY SERVE
LOCKERS—A POPULAR CHATTING PLACE) SHOULD
PROVIDE THE MODEL BUILDER WITH ORIENTATION.

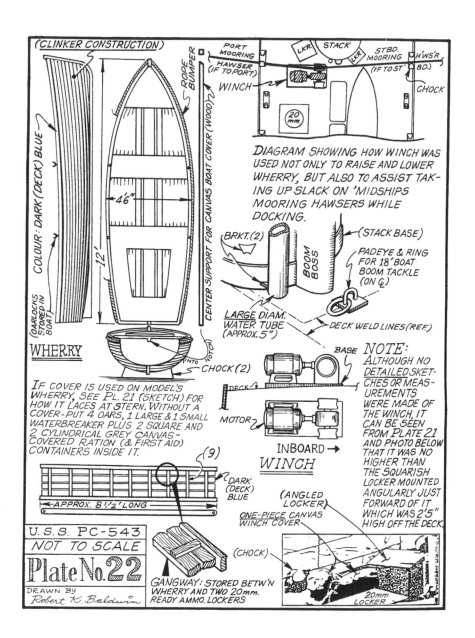

(CLINKER CONSTRUCTION)

COLOUR: DARK (DECK) BLUE

ROPE BUMPER

CENTER SUPPORT FOR CANVAS BOAT COVER (WOOD)

4'6"

12'

(OARLOCKS STORED IN BOAT)

WHERRY

INTO NOTCH

IF COVER IS USED ON MODEL'S WHERRY, SEE PL.21 (SKETCH) FOR HOW IT LACES AT STERN. WITHOUT A COVER - PUT 4 OARS, 1 LARGE & 1 SMALL WATERBREAKER PLUS 2 SQUARE AND 2 CYLINDRICAL GREY CANVAS-COVERED RATION (& FIRST AID) CONTAINERS INSIDE IT.

PORT MOORING
HAWSER (IF TO PORT)
WINCH
LKR STACK LKR
STBD. MOORING (IF TO ST')
H'WS'R (BD.)
CHOCK
20 mm

DIAGRAM SHOWING HOW WINCH WAS USED NOT ONLY TO RAISE AND LOWER WHERRY, BUT ALSO TO ASSIST TAKING UP SLACK ON 'MIDSHIPS MOORING HAWSERS WHILE DOCKING.

BRKT.(2)
BOOM BOSS
(STACK BASE)
PADEYE & RING FOR 18' BOAT BOOM TACKLE (ON ℄)

LARGE DIAM. WATER TUBE (APPROX. 5")
DECK WELD LINES (REF.)

CHOCK (2)

DECK
MOTOR
BASE
INBOARD →
WINCH

NOTE:
ALTHOUGH NO DETAILED SKETCHES OR MEASUREMENTS WERE MADE OF THE WINCH, IT CAN BE SEEN FROM PLATE 21 AND PHOTO BELOW THAT IT WAS NO HIGHER THAN THE SQUARISH LOCKER MOUNTED ANGULARLY JUST FORWARD OF IT WHICH WAS 2'5" HIGH OFF THE DECK.

(9)
DARK (DECK) BLUE
← APPROX. 8½' LONG →

(ANGLED LOCKER)
ONE-PIECE CANVAS WINCH COVER
(CHOCK)

U.S.S. PC-543
NOT TO SCALE
Plate No. 22
DRAWN BY
Robert K. Baldwin

GANGWAY: STORED BETW'N WHERRY AND TWO 20mm. READY AMMO. LOCKERS

20mm LOCKER

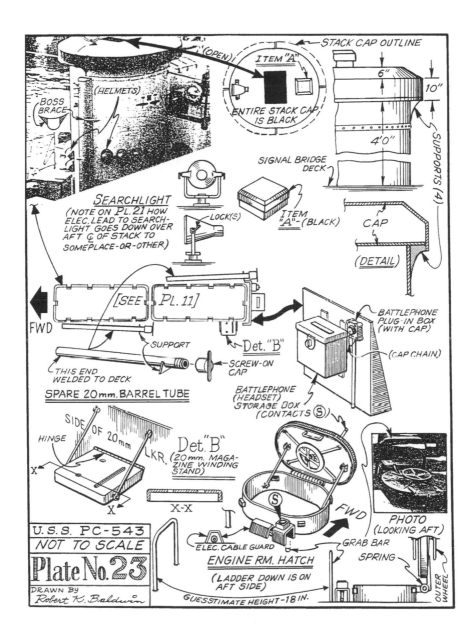

STACK CAP OUTLINE

(OPEN)

ITEM "A"

ENTIRE STACK CAP IS BLACK

6"

10"

4'0"

SUPPORTS (4)

(HELMETS)

BOSS BRACE

SIGNAL BRIDGE DECK

CAP

(DETAIL)

SEARCHLIGHT
(NOTE ON PL. 21 HOW ELEC. LEAD TO SEARCHLIGHT GOES DOWN OVER AFT ℄ OF STACK TO SOMEPLACE-OR-OTHER)

LOCK(S)

ITEM "A" - (BLACK)

[SEE PL. 11]

FWD

SUPPORT

Det."B"

SCREW-ON CAP

THIS END WELDED TO DECK

SPARE 20mm. BARREL TUBE

BATTLEPHONE PLUG-IN BOX (WITH CAP)

(CAP CHAIN)

BATTLEPHONE (HEADSET) STORAGE BOX (CONTACTS Ⓢ)

SIDE OF 20mm

HINGE

Det. "B"
(20mm. MAGAZINE WINDING STAND)

X

LKR.

X

X-X

FWD

PHOTO (LOOKING AFT)

U.S.S. PC-543
NOT TO SCALE

Plate No. 23

DRAWN BY
Robert K. Baldwin

ELEC. CABLE GUARD

ENGINE RM. HATCH
(LADDER DOWN IS ON AFT SIDE)

GUESSTIMATE HEIGHT-18 IN.

GRAB BAR

SPRING

OUTER WHEEL

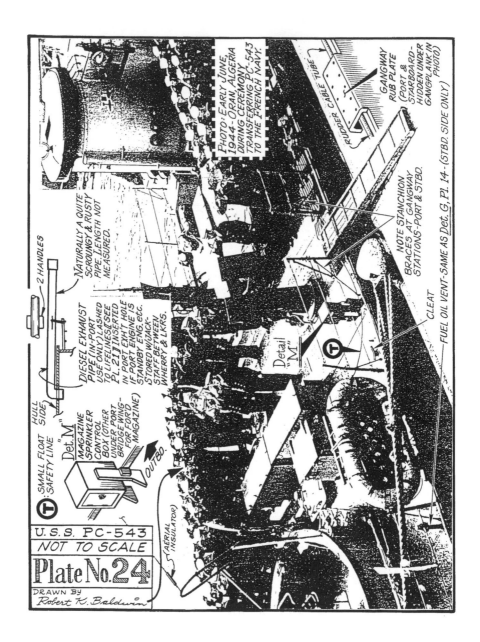

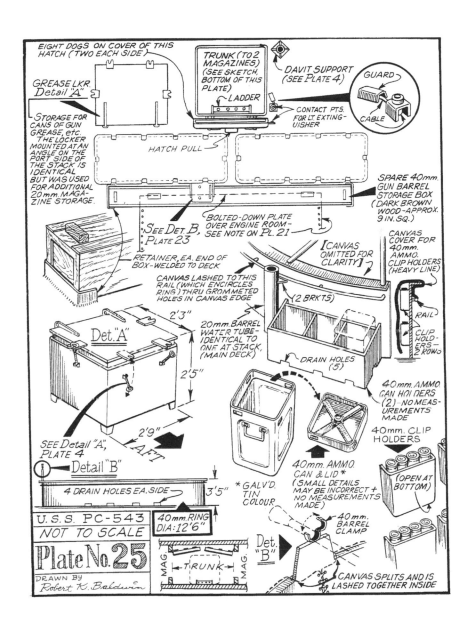

EIGHT DOGS ON COVER OF THIS HATCH (TWO EACH SIDE)

TRUNK (TO 2 MAGAZINES) (SEE SKETCH, BOTTOM OF THIS PLATE)

DAVIT SUPPORT (SEE PLATE 4)

GUARD

CABLE

GREASE LKR. Detail "A"

LADDER

CONTACT PTS. FOR LT. EXTINGUISHER

STORAGE FOR CANS OF GUN GREASE, etc. THE LOCKER MOUNTED AT AN ANGLE ON THE PORT SIDE OF THE STACK IS IDENTICAL BUT WAS USED FOR ADDITIONAL 20mm. MAGAZINE STORAGE.

HATCH PULL

SPARE 40mm. GUN BARREL STORAGE BOX (DARK BROWN WOOD-APPROX. 9 IN. SQ.)

SEE DET. B, PLATE 23

BOLTED-DOWN PLATE OVER ENGINE ROOM- SEE NOTE ON PL. 21

CANVAS COVER FOR 40mm. AMMO. CLIP HOLDERS (HEAVY LINE)

RETAINER, EA. END OF BOX-WELDED TO DECK

[CANVAS OMITTED FOR CLARITY]

CANVAS LASHED TO THIS RAIL (WHICH ENCIRCLES RING) THRU GROMMETED HOLES IN CANVAS EDGE

(2 BRKTS.)

RAIL

CLIP HOLDERS- 2 ROWS

Det. "A"

2'3"

20mm. BARREL WATER TUBE- IDENTICAL TO ONE AT STACK, (MAIN DECK)

2'5"

DRAIN HOLES (5)

40mm. AMMO. CAN HOLDERS (2) -NO MEASUREMENTS MADE

40mm. CLIP HOLDERS

2'9"

AFT

SEE Detail "A", PLATE 4

Detail "B"

40mm. AMMO. CAN & LID * (SMALL DETAILS MAY BE INCORRECT + NO MEASUREMENTS MADE)

(OPEN AT BOTTOM)

4 DRAIN HOLES EA. SIDE

3'5"

* GALV'D. TIN COLOUR

U.S.S. PC-543

NOT TO SCALE

40mm. RING DIA: 12'6"

40mm. BARREL CLAMP

Plate No. 25

DRAWN BY Robert K. Baldwin

MAG. TRUNK MAG.

Det. "B"

CANVAS SPLITS AND IS LASHED TOGETHER INSIDE

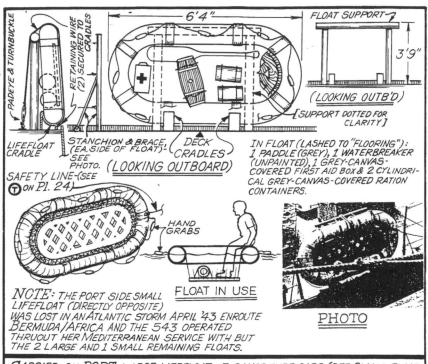

6'4"

FLOAT SUPPORT

PADEYE & TURNBUCKLE

RETAINING WIRE (2) SECURED TO CRADLES

3'9"

(LOOKING OUTB'D)

[SUPPORT DOTTED FOR CLARITY]

LIFEFLOAT CRADLE

STANCHION & BRACE, (EA. SIDE OF FLOAT)- SEE PHOTO.

DECK CRADLES

(LOOKING OUTBOARD)

IN FLOAT (LASHED TO "FLOORING"): 1 PADDLE (GREY), 1 WATERBREAKER (UNPAINTED), 1 GREY-CANVAS-COVERED FIRST AID BOX & 2 CYLINDRICAL GREY-CANVAS-COVERED RATION CONTAINERS.

SAFETY LINE-(SEE Ⓣ on Pl. 24)

HAND GRABS

FLOAT IN USE

NOTE: THE PORT SIDE SMALL LIFEFLOAT (DIRECTLY OPPOSITE) WAS LOST IN AN ATLANTIC STORM APRIL '43 ENROUTE BERMUDA/AFRICA AND THE 543 OPERATED THRUOUT HER MEDITERRANEAN SERVICE WITH BUT THE 2 LARGE AND 1 SMALL REMAINING FLOATS.

<u>PHOTO</u>

CARRIED ON <u>PORT</u> LARGE LIFEFLOAT: 3 CANOE-TYPE OARS (SEE <u>SMALL</u> FLOAT DWG-TOP OF THIS PLATE), 2 LARGE WATERBREAKERS, 1 FOLDED CANVAS TARPAULIN, 2 CYLINDRICAL EMERG. RATION CONTAINERS AND 1 SQUARE FIRST AID BOX (W/RED CROSS THEREON)-LAST THREE ITEMS COVERED W/ GREY CANVAS.

CARRIED ON <u>STBD.</u> LARGE LIFEFLOAT: 3 OARS (SAME), 2 WATERBREAKERS, 1 LARGE RECTANGULAR & 1 CYLINDRICAL RATION CONTAINER PLUS A FIRST AID BOX & A FOLDED TARPAULIN. ALL ITEMS LASHED <u>INBOARD</u> (TOP OF FLOAT'S "FLOORING") SO THAT WHEN FLOAT IS RELEASED OVERBOARD ITEMS WILL BE ACCESSIBLE TO OCCUPANTS.

As two seamen man the gun, another winds up the magazine for the 20mm AA cannon aboard a PC. The winding operation results in the shells being forced into the breech, thus keeping the gun firing.

U.S.S. PC-543

NOT TO SCALE

(PHOTO FROM "OUR NAVY" MAGAZINE)

WINDING LEVER

Plate No. 26

DRAWN BY
Robert K. Baldwin

20mm. MAGAZINE IN A WINDING STAND SUCH AS THAT SHOWN ON EITHER PLATES 11 OR 23.

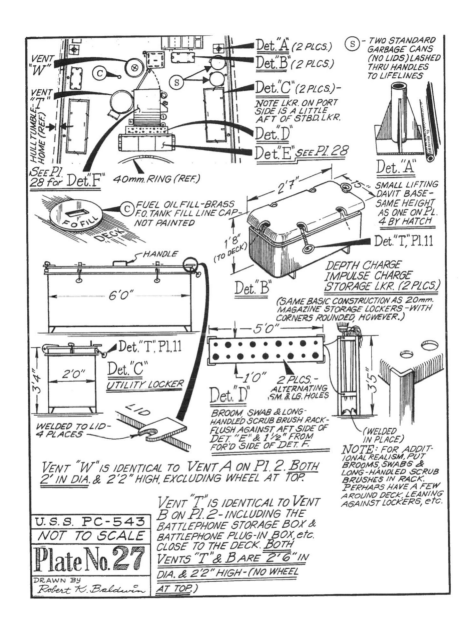

VENT "W"

VENT "T"

HULL TUMBLE-HOME (REF.)

SEE Pl. 28 for Det."F"

Det."A" (2 PLCS.)
Det."B" (2 PLCS.)

Det."C" (2 PLCS.)-
NOTE LKR. ON PORT SIDE IS A LITTLE AFT OF STBD. LKR.

Det."D"
Det."E" SEE Pl. 28

Ⓢ - TWO STANDARD GARBAGE CANS (NO LIDS) LASHED THRU HANDLES TO LIFELINES

Det."A"
SMALL LIFTING DAVIT BASE- SAME HEIGHT AS ONE ON Pl. 4 BY HATCH

40mm. RING (REF.)

Ⓒ FUEL OIL FILL-BRASS F.O. TANK FILL LINE CAP- NOT PAINTED

FO FILL   DECK

2'7"

1'8" (TO DECK)

Det."B"

Det."T", Pl. 11

DEPTH CHARGE IMPULSE CHARGE STORAGE LKR. (2 PLCS.)
(SAME BASIC CONSTRUCTION AS 20mm. MAGAZINE STORAGE LOCKERS - WITH CORNERS ROUNDED, HOWEVER.)

HANDLE

6'0"

Det."T", Pl. 11
Det."C"
UTILITY LOCKER

3'4"   2'0"

WELDED TO LID- 4 PLACES

LID

5'0"

1'0"   2 PLCS.- ALTERNATING SM. & LG. HOLES
Det."D"

BROOM, SWAB & LONG- HANDLED SCRUB BRUSH RACK- FLUSH AGAINST AFT SIDE OF DET."E" & 1½" FROM FOR'D SIDE OF DET. F.

3'5"

(WELDED IN PLACE)

NOTE: FOR ADDIT- IONAL REALISM, PUT BROOMS, SWABS & LONG-HANDLED SCRUB BRUSHES IN RACK. PERHAPS HAVE A FEW AROUND DECK, LEANING AGAINST LOCKERS, etc.

VENT "W" IS IDENTICAL TO VENT A ON Pl. 2. BOTH 2' IN DIA. & 2'2" HIGH, EXCLUDING WHEEL AT TOP.

VENT "T" IS IDENTICAL TO VENT B ON Pl. 2 - INCLUDING THE BATTLEPHONE STORAGE BOX & BATTLEPHONE PLUG-IN BOX, etc. CLOSE TO THE DECK. BOTH VENTS "T" & B ARE 2'6" IN DIA. & 2'2" HIGH - (NO WHEEL AT TOP.)

U.S.S. PC-543
NOT TO SCALE
Plate No. 27
DRAWN BY
Robert K. Baldwin

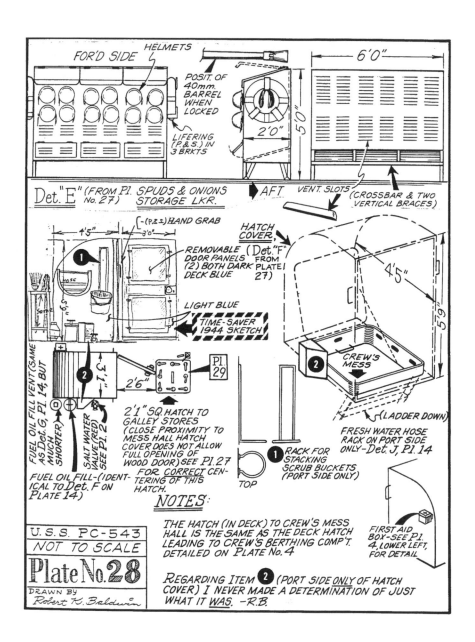

FOR'D SIDE   HELMETS

POSIT. OF
40mm.
BARREL
WHEN
LOCKED

LIFE RING
(P.&S.) IN
3 BRKTS

6'0"

5'0"

2'0"

Det."E" (FROM Pl. SPUDS & ONIONS
          No.27)   STORAGE LKR.

AFT   VENT. SLOTS (CROSSBAR & TWO
                          VERTICAL BRACES)

-(P.&±) HAND GRAB

4'5"   3'0"

REMOVABLE (Det."F"
DOOR PANELS FROM
(2) BOTH DARK PLATE
DECK BLUE   27)

HATCH
COVER

LIGHT BLUE

TIME-SAVER
1944 SKETCH

4'5"

5'9"

CREW'S
MESS

Pl
29

2'6"

3'1"

FUEL OIL FILL VENT (SAME
AS Det. G, Pl. 14, BUT
MUCH SHORTER)

SALT WATER
VALVE (RED)
SEE Pl. 2

FUEL OIL FILL-(IDENT-
ICAL TO Det. F ON
PLATE 14)

2'1" SQ. HATCH TO
GALLEY STORES
(CLOSE PROXIMITY TO
MESS HALL HATCH
COVER DOES NOT ALLOW
FULL OPENING OF
WOOD DOOR) SEE Pl.27
FOR CORRECT CEN-
TERING OF THIS
HATCH.

TOP

RACK FOR
STACKING
SCRUB BUCKETS
(PORT SIDE ONLY)

(LADDER DOWN)

FRESH WATER HOSE
RACK ON PORT SIDE
ONLY-Det. J, Pl. 14

NOTES:

U.S.S. PC-543
NOT TO SCALE

Plate No. 28

DRAWN BY
Robert K. Baldwin

THE HATCH (IN DECK) TO CREW'S MESS
HALL IS THE SAME AS THE DECK HATCH
LEADING TO CREW'S BERTHING COMP'T.
DETAILED ON PLATE No.4

FIRST AID
BOX-SEE Pl.
4, LOWER LEFT,
FOR DETAIL

REGARDING ITEM **2** (PORT SIDE ONLY OF HATCH
COVER) I NEVER MADE A DETERMINATION OF JUST
WHAT IT WAS. -R.B.

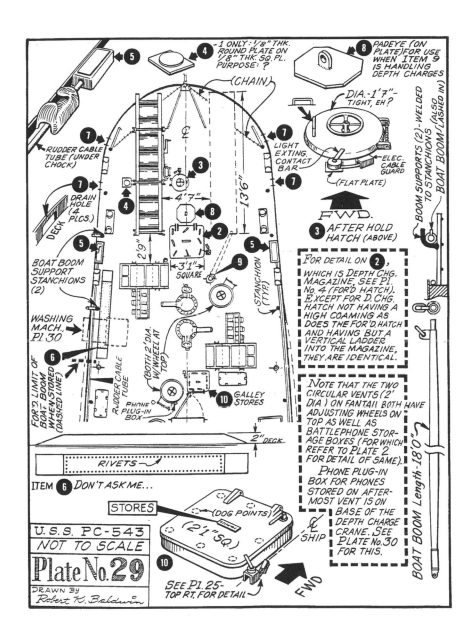

-1 ONLY - 1/8" THK. ROUND PLATE ON 1/8" THK. SQ. PL. PURPOSE: ?

⑧ PADEYE (ON PLATE) FOR USE WHEN ITEM 9 IS HANDLING DEPTH CHARGES

(CHAIN)

DIA. - 1'7"- TIGHT, EH?

⑦ RUDDER CABLE TUBE (UNDER CHOCK)

LIGHT EXTING. CONTACT BAR

ELEC. CABLE GUARD

DRAIN HOLE (4 PLCS.)

③ LIGHT EXTING. CONTACT BAR

4'7"

13'6"

(FLAT PLATE)

FWD.

③ AFTER HOLD HATCH (ABOVE)

DECK

② BOAT BOOM SUPPORT STANCHIONS (2)

2'9"

3'1" SQUARE

⑨ STANCHION (TYP.)

BOOM SUPPORTS (2) - WELDED TO STANCHIONS
BOAT BOOM (ALSO LASHED IN)

WASHING MACH., Pl. 30

(BOTH 2' DIA. W/ WHEEL AT TOP)

FOR'D. LIMIT OF BOAT BOOM WHEN STORED (DASHED LINE)

⑥

RUDDER CABLE TUBE

PHONE PLUG-IN BOX

⑩ GALLEY STORES

For detail on ②, which is depth chg. magazine, see Pl. No. 4 (for'd hatch). Except for d. chg. hatch not having a high coaming as does the for'd hatch and having but a vertical ladder into the magazine, they are identical.

Note that the two circular vents (2' dia.) on fantail both have adjusting wheels on top as well as battlephone storage boxes (for which refer to plate 2 for detail of same).

Phone plug-in box for phones stored on after-most vent is on base of the depth charge crane. See plate No. 30 for this.

2" DECK

RIVETS

ITEM ⑥ Don't ask me...

STORES

(DOG POINTS)

(2'1" SQ.)

U.S.S. PC-543
NOT TO SCALE
Plate No. 29
DRAWN BY
Robert K. Baldwin

⑩ SEE Pl. 25 - TOP RT. FOR DETAIL

FWD

Ç SHIP

BOAT BOOM Length-18'0"

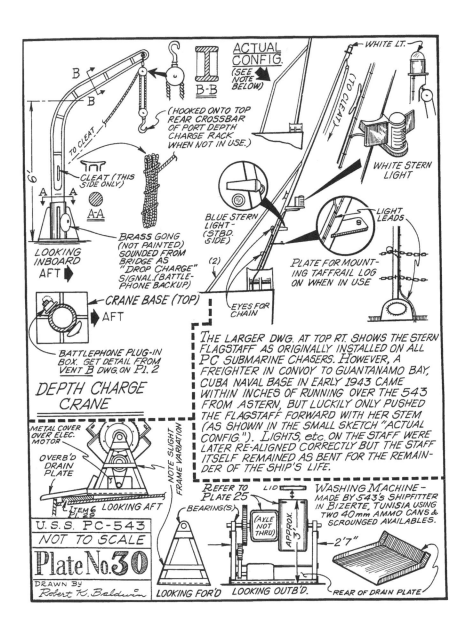

ACTUAL CONFIG. (SEE NOTE BELOW)

B-B

← WHITE LT.

(TO CLEAT)

B
B

(HOOKED ONTO TOP REAR CROSSBAR OF PORT DEPTH CHARGE RACK WHEN NOT IN USE.)

TO CLEAT

CLEAT (THIS SIDE ONLY)

A A

A-A

6'

WHITE STERN LIGHT

LOOKING INBOARD
AFT ▶

BRASS GONG (NOT PAINTED) SOUNDED FROM BRIDGE AS "DROP CHARGE" SIGNAL. (BATTLE-PHONE BACKUP)

BLUE STERN LIGHT – (STBD. SIDE)

(2)

LIGHT LEADS

PLATE FOR MOUNT-ING TAFFRAIL LOG ON WHEN IN USE

CRANE BASE (TOP)
▶ AFT

EYES FOR CHAIN

BATTLEPHONE PLUG-IN BOX. GET DETAIL FROM VENT B DWG. ON Pl. 2

DEPTH CHARGE CRANE

The LARGER DWG. AT TOP RT. SHOWS THE STERN FLAGSTAFF AS ORIGINALLY INSTALLED ON ALL PC SUBMARINE CHASERS. HOWEVER, A FREIGHTER IN CONVOY TO GUANTANAMO BAY, CUBA NAVAL BASE IN EARLY 1943 CAME WITHIN INCHES OF RUNNING OVER THE 543 FROM ASTERN, BUT LUCKILY ONLY PUSHED THE FLAGSTAFF FORWARD WITH HER STEM (AS SHOWN IN THE SMALL SKETCH "ACTUAL CONFIG."). LIGHTS, etc. ON THE STAFF WERE LATER RE-ALIGNED CORRECTLY BUT THE STAFF ITSELF REMAINED AS BENT FOR THE REMAIN-DER OF THE SHIP'S LIFE.

METAL COVER OVER ELEC. MOTOR

OVERB'D DRAIN PLATE

NOTE SLIGHT FRAME VARIATION

ITEM 6 LOOKING AFT

REFER TO PLATE 25

LID

BEARING(S)

(AXLE NOT THRU)

APPROX. 3'

WASHING MACHINE – MADE BY 543's SHIPFITTER IN BIZERTE, TUNISIA USING TWO 40mm AMMO CANS & SCROUNGED AVAILABLES.

2'7"

U.S.S. PC-543
NOT TO SCALE
Plate No. 30
DRAWN BY
Robert K. Baldwin

LOOKING FOR'D   LOOKING OUTB'D.

REAR OF DRAIN PLATE

BIBLIOGRAPHY

NONFICTION

1. Andrade, Allan, *S. S. Leopoldville Disaster* (The Tern Book Co., New York, 1997).

2. Baker, A. D., III, "Historic Fleets," <u>Naval History</u>, Page 62, U. S. Naval Institute, January-February 1996.

3. Bell, Art, *Peter Charlie – The Cruise of the PC477* (Courtroom Compendiums, Woodland Hills, California, 1982).

4. Bishop, Eleanor C., *Prints in the Sand: The U.S. Coast Guard Beach Patrol During World War II* (Pictorial Histories Publishing Co. Inc., 1989).

5. *Bluejackets' Manual, The*, United States Navy, Tenth Edition (United States Naval Institute, Annapolis, Maryland, 1940).

6. Elliott, P., *Allied Escort Ships of World War II* (Macdonald and Jane's Publishers Limited, London, 1977).

7. Elliott, Peter, *Allied Minesweeping in World War 2* (Patrick Stephens, Ltd., 1979).

8. Fahey, James. C., *The Ships and Aircraft of the United States Fleet, 1945*, four volumes, Reprint (Naval Institute Press, Annapolis, Maryland, 1976).

9. Friedman, Norman, *U. S. Small Combatants* (US Naval Institute, Annapolis, Maryland, 1987).

10. Garfield, Brian, *The Thousand Mile War – World War II in Alaska and the Aleutians* (Doubleday and Co., Inc., New York, 1969).

11. Holland, W. J., Jr., RAdm, USN (Ret), *The Navy* (Naval Historical Foundation, Washington, D. C., 2000).

12. *Janes' Fighting Ships of World War II, 1939-1945*, reprint (Studio Editions, Ltd., London, 1989.)

13. Johnson, Ellis A. and David A. Katcher, *Mines Against Japan* (Silver Spring, Maryland, Naval Ordnance Laboratory, 1973).

14. Johnson, Robert Erwin *Guardians of the Sea: History of the United States Coast Guard, 1915 to the Present* (United States Naval Institute, Annapolis, Maryland, April 1988).

15. Johnson, Robert Erwin, *Bering Sea Escort – Life Aboard a Coast Guard Cutter in World War II* (Naval Institute Press, Annapolis, Maryland, 1992).

16. Lambert, John and Al Ross, *Allied Coastal Forced of World War II, Volume 1, Fairmile Designs and US Submarine Chasers* (Naval Institute Press, Annapolis, Maryland, 1994).

17. Lenton, H. T. And J. J. Colledge, *Warships of World War II* (Ian Allan, 1965).

18. Lewis, David D., *The Fight for the Sea – The Past, Present, and Future of Submarine Warfare in the Atlantic* (The World Publishing Co., New York, 1961).

19. Lott, Arnold S., *Most Dangerous Sea: A History of Mine Warfare and an Account of U.S. Navy Mine Warfare Operations in World War II and Korea* (U.S. Naval Institute, Annapolis, Maryland, 1959).

20. Mann, Earl, Appendix to *Dictionary of American Naval Fighting Ships, Vol. VI*, Office of CNO, Naval History Div., Washington, D.C. Rough Draft, Private Communication from CDR Earl Mann, 4 January 1971.

21. Morison, Samuel L., *Guide to Naval Mine Warfare*, Edited by Jeff W. Schomisch (Pasha Publications, Incorporated,1995).

22. Morison, Samuel Eliot, *History of United States Naval Operations in WWII, Volumes I–XV* (Little, Brown and Company, Boston, Massachusetts, 1947 and later dates).

23. Morison, Samuel Eliot, *The Two–Ocean War, a Short History of the United States Navy in the Second World War* (Little, Brown and Company, Boston, Massachusetts, 1963).

24. *Patrol Craft Sailors Association History Book* (Turner Publishing Co., Paducah, 1990).

25. *Patrol Craft Sailors Association History Book* (Turner Publishing Co., Paducah, 1995).

26.Purdon, Eric, *Black Company – The story of Subchaser 1264* (Robert B. Luce, Inc., New York, 1972).

27. Roberts, Douglas L., *Rustbucket 7, Chronicle of the USS PC 617 During the Great War, 1942 – 1946* (Mill Pond Press, New Castle, Maine, 1995).

28. Scheina, Robert L., *U.S. Coast Guard Cutters and Craft: 1946-1990* (United States Naval Institute, Annapolis, Maryland, 1990).

29. Scheina, Robert L., *U. S. Coast Guard Cutters & Craft of World War II* (Naval Institute Press, Annapolis, Maryland, 1982).

30. Schultz, James R., *The Long Way Home – A Pacific Odyssey of WWII* (Creative Arts Book Co., Berkeley, 1996).

31. Silverstone, Paul H., *U. S. Warships of World War II* (Doubleday & Company, Inc., New York, 1965).

32. Stafford, Edward P., *Subchaser* (Warner Books, Inc., New York, 1988).

33. Submarine Chaser Manual 1942 Second Edition (Restricted), U. S. Navy Department, Declassified. Library of Congress, F. A. C. File No. 642, November 14, 1957 (United States Government Printing Office, Washington, 1942).

34. Treadwell, Theodore R., *Splinter Fleet – The Wooden Subchasers of World War II* (Naval Institute Press, Annapolis, Maryland, 2000).

35. United States Naval Chronology, World War II, Naval History Division, Office of the Chief of Naval Operations, Navy Department, Washington, D. C., 1955.

36. "United States Naval Vessels Lost During the War," Press and Radio Release, Navy Department, 2 October 1945.

37. Veigele, Wm. J., *PC Patrol Craft of World War II – A History of the Ships and Their Crews* (Astral Publishing Co., Santa Barbara, California, 1998).

38. Watts, Anthony, *The U-Boat Hunters* (Purnell Book Services, Ltd., 1976).

39. Willoughby, Malcolm, F., *The U. S. Coast Guard in World War II* , Revised Printing (Naval Institute Press, Annapolis, Maryland, 1989).

FICTION

1. Hall, Wesley, *The Splendid five – A True Story About the Splinter Fleet in the Pacific During WWII* (Writers Club Press, New York, 2000).

2. Jonnes, Nelson, *How PC-620 Won the War in the Pacific – an Account of the famous April Fool's Day sinking of the Japanese Battleship YUNUSUZI* (Jonnes Research Company, 15320 North 113th Street, Stillwater, Minnesota, 55082, 1994).

3. McCarthy, Jack, *Winners Also Cry* (Vantage Press, New York, 1996).

4. McKay, James, *Bill Creelman's Conflicts – A Story of A Boy's Coming of Age* (James McKay, 2000).

5. Miller, Roderick, *The Ship With No Name – PCE 855* (Van Tag Press, Inc., New York, 2001).

6. Reeman, Douglas, *Path of the Storm – Terror in the China Seas* (G. P. Putnam's Sons, New York, 1966).

FILM LIBRARY

This collection of films about the United States Navy and Coast Guard in World War II and small craft includes a commercial movie, a commercial video tape, government films from the National Archives, and personal video tapes.

COMMERCIAL MOVIE

"You're in the Navy Now." The 20th Century Fox Film Corporation made this film in 1951. It starred Gary Cooper, Jane Greer, and other yet to be famous actors. It is a fictionalized account of PC 452, called USS *Teakettle*. This ship had an experimental steam engine installed. The experiment failed and the Navy used Diesel engines in all other PCs.

COMMERCIAL VIDEO TAPES

"Great Lakes, NTC." This video, available from Military History Videos, shows training at the Great Lakes Naval Training Station (Boot Camp) in Illinois in the 1940s.

"Coast Guard Battle Action in World War II." Available from Military History Videos.

"Beachhead to Berlin: Coast Guard's Role in the Normandy Invasion." Available from Military History Videos.

NATIONAL ARCHIVE FILMS

The national archives in Washington, DC contains many films of World War II including naval actions. Many of the films have segments showing small ships in action. Information on twenty-five of these films may be obtained from the Archives, the author, or Jim Heywood of the Patrol Craft Sailors Association.

PERSONAL VIDEO TAPES

Some former small ship sailors obtained movie and video footage of ships from various sources and put it together in video tapes. Those films and videos known to the author and in his possession are listed below.

1. Six Royal Thai Navy PCs in 1969. The Thai Navy PC No. 4 was formerly USS PC 1585.
2. PCs 479, 1181, 1183, 555.
3. PC 1064.
4. PC 1264. Also of PC 1230 at the Peleliu invasion.
5. Commissioning of PC 1264.
6. "A PC Story" by Bob Daly, a history.
7. About PC 472 by Joe Luteran.
8. Launch of PC 451.
9. PC 543 under construction at the Defoe Shipbuilding Co.
10. Bob Daly, miscellaneous views and information about PCs.
11. PCSA Reunions 1999 and 2000.
12. PC 566, tour of AM 240 in May 2001, Newsreels from 1944, and views of PC 609.
13. Ship Models by Robert Raymond, a tour of ship models and making ship models.
14. Interview with Capt. Joe Peck (USN Ret) about experiences as Commanding Officer of PC 1122.

RELATED WEBSITES

NAVY WEBSITES

1. www.history.navy.mil/faqs/faq82-1.html
This section of the Naval Historical Center website includes casualties of WWII U. S. Navy and Coast Guard vessels including various types of patrol craft.

2. http://navsource.org/archives/home.html
This website claims to have the largest collection of photographs of US Navy warships on the internet.

3. http://groups.msn.com/worldwarIIclub/pictures
This site contains photographs of World War II including Navy and Coast Guard ships.

4. www.ibiblio.org/hyperwar/index.html#usn
This Hyper War hypertext history of World War II website displays data on ships of the United States Navy during the period 1940-45.

5. www.hazegray.org
This website contains general naval information about the world's navies.

6. www.history.navy.mil
This is the official website of the Naval Historical Center and has general naval information and links to other sites.

7. www.seahistory.org/public_html/frame.htm
    This is the website of the National Maritime Historical Society and contains general information and links.

8. www.mediacen.navy.mil
    This is the website of the Naval Media Center and contains navy information and links.

9. www.mediacen.navy.mil/pubs/allhands/an00/ pg32b.htm#patrol
    This section of the Naval Media Center has information on current navy ships.

10. www.nvr.navy.mil/nvrships/index.htm
    This Naval Vessel Register site contains information on all U. S. Navy ships.

11. www.lonesailor.org
    This is the website for the U. S. Navy Memorial Foundation. It has much information and links to other sites.

12. www.ncts.navy.mil/nol
    This site has a list of links to Navy sites worldwide.

COAST GUARD WEBSITES

13. www.uss-seaweed.com
    This site has Army, Navy, and Coast Guard histories and photographs.

14. www.uscg.mil/uscg.shtm
    This is the home page of the United States Coast Guard.

15. www.uscg.mil/hg/g-cp/history/h_cgnvy.html
    This site is about the United States Navy vessels manned by the United States Coast Guard in World War II.

16. www.aug.edu/~libwrw/cgcva/cgcva.htm
    This is a Coast Guard Combat Veterans Association site that has interesting material and links to other sites.

17. http://home.earthlink.net/~kenlong1942/cgsva.html
    This is a site for the Coast Guard Sea Veterans of America.

18. www.ibiblio.org/hyperwar/usn
    This website describes the U. S. Navy in World War II and includes the Coast Guard. It has links to other sites.

19. www.fcgh.org
    This is the website of the Foundation for Coast Guard History. It has links to many sites.

20. www.uscgaparents.org/links
    This site has general information and links to other sites,

NAVAL MINE WARFARE WEBSITES
21. http://hometown.aol.com/fredricxxx
    This is a site for the Naval Mine Warfare Association started by the members of the Pearl Harbor Survivors Association.

22. http://home.triad.rr.com/aom/index.htm
    This is the site of the Association of Minemen. It is devoted to mine warfare.
23. http://www.ae.utexas.edu/~industry/mine/
    This is the Unofficial Mine Warfare Home Page. It has links to other sites.

24. www.pioneer.navy.mil/minw_warfare.htm
        This site has a general discussion of mine warfare and a list of United States ports mined during World War II.

25. http://hometown.aol.com/fredricxxx/history.htm
        This site recounts the history of mine warfare vessel classifications.

NATIONAL ARCHIVE WEBSITES

26. http://monitor.nara.gov
        This is the website of the National Archives and Records Administration. The archives contains much information on World War II and U. S. Navy ships.

**27. http://monitor.nara.gov/publications/sl/
navyships/patrol.html**
        This section of the National Archives and Records Administration website displays information on patrol craft.

FOREIGN SHIP WEBSITES

28. www.lioncity.com.tw/cwn/taiwan/4203.html
        This Republic of China (Taiwan) website shows photographs and lists data for WWII PCs that were transferred to their navy.

**29. www.history.navy.mil/photos/sh-fornv/rok/roksh-
mr/paktusn.htm**
        This section of the Naval Historical Center website shows photographs and gives information on PC 701 in the Navy of the Republic of Korea (South Korea).

30. www.history.navy.mil/photos/sh-fornv/rok/roksh-sz/samksn.htm

This section of the Naval Historical Center website shows photographs and gives information on PC 703 in the Navy of the Republic of Korea (South Korea).

31. www.history.navy.mil/photos/sh-fornv/rok/roksh-ag/chirisn.htm

This section of the Naval Historical Center website shows photographs and gives information on PC 704 in the Navy of the Republic of Korea (South Korea).

PRIVATELY OPERATED WEBSITES

32. www.ww2pcsa.org

This is the website of the Patrol Craft Sailors Association (PCSA). It contains descriptions and photographs of small ships and membership information for the PCSA.

33. www.astralpublishing.com

This website contains information on and a link to the book *PC Patrol Craft of World War II*. It also has links to other Navy websites.

34. http://members.aol.com/diodor/splinterfleet

This website is about the SC subchasers of World War II. It also gives links to a book about SCs and other Navy websites.

35. www.boat-links.combat/boatlinks.html

This website claims to be "The mother of all maritime links." It has many links to naval related websites.

36. www.geocities.com/friedkappes/flagship.html
      This site contains naval related photographs, links, information, and posts.

37. http://goatlocker.exis.net/seabag.htm
      This personal website contains a humorous account of what a Navy Sea Bag meant to a sailor.

38. www.jacksjoint.com/cglinks.htm
      Many Coast Guard links are on this website along with general information about the Coast Guard.

SHIP MODELING WEBSITES

38. www.paperlab.com
      This site is for Paper-Lab Publishing a Canadian firm that makes and sells paper ship models.

39. www.brown.abelgratis.co.uk
      This small warship website has information on models of small ships.

40. www.smmlonline.com
      This is the site of the Ship Modeling Mailing List (SMML). It has articles, kit and book reviews, photographs, and links to other sites. The mailing list is a contributor's site open to subscribers (free), and presents discussions of modeling and other naval and maritime related issues.

COLOR PLATES

This section contains twenty-six plates in color. They are copies of paintings and other items made by small ship sailors and persons associated with them. Some were made during and some after World War II. Their titles, artists, contributors, dates, mediums, and other information about them are listed here in the order in which the paintings appear on the following pages. After each entry is the Figure number used in the text that includes a caption with information about, acknowledgment for, and permission to use the item.

1. In Port for R and R, Oil Painting, Jim Kennedy. Figure XII-16.
2. Top View of a PC Underway, Oil Painting, Jim Kennedy. Figure XII-14.
3. Moonlight Convoy, Oil Painting, Jim Kennedy. Figure XII-15.
4. Rough Riding, Oil Painting, Jim Kennedy. Figure XII-13.
5. PC 616, Oil Painting. Sid Frey. Figure V-5.
6. Cutaway drawing of SC 497, Color added by computer, David P. Lawrence, 1997. Figure X-10.
7. U. S. O., Tunis, Tunisia, N. W. Africa, Water Color, George Amaral, 1943. Figure V-14.
8. French Army Base, Tenes, Tunisia, W. Africa, Water Color, George Amaral, 1943. Figure IV-19.

9. Model of PGM 18, Joe Kelliher and Tom Pollock, 1994. Figure XII-24.

10. Man in Water Watching His Ship Sink, PC 496, Oil Painting, Carter Barber. Figure IX-7.

11. Arab Sheik, N. W. Africa, Water Color, George Amaral, 1944. Figure IV-21.

12. Muslim Woman, N. W. Africa, Water Color, George Amaral,1944. Figure IV-22.

13. Arab Dancer and Arab With Fez, N. W. Africa, Water Color, George Amaral, 1944. Figure IV-20.

14. PC Attacking a German U-Boat, Tempera Water-based Paint, Joe Luca, 1950. Figure XII-27.

15. Zootsuit Man, Water Color, Robert S. Laurie. Figure V-12.

16. Zootsuit Man and Girl, Water Color, Robert S. Laurie. Figure V-13.

17. Signet for PC 1178, William Tormey. Figure XII-28.

18. Model of W 26 in Haze Gray, Michel Lelievre. Figure X-9.

19. Donald Duck Coast Guard Corsair Insignia, National Archives. Figure VIII-1.

20. Donald Duck Patch. Figure I-6.

21. Painting of YP 478, Water Color, James H. Byington. Property of the Bay County Historical Society, used with permission. Figure VII-5.

22. Model of SC 648, Theodore Treadwell. Figure XII-23.

23. "Augie," stack art on AM 242, Marker Pen, J. M. Passmann,. Figure VII-6.

24. Replica of a ship's wheel or helm. It was made of miscellaneous parts, Donald R. Hatfield. Figure XII-19.

25. "Ruptured Duck" Discharge Emblem for wearing on a uniform. Figure XI-2.

26. Commemorative Community Program Logo of the PCSA. Figure XII-4.

Color Plates 1 and 2

Color Plates 3 and 4

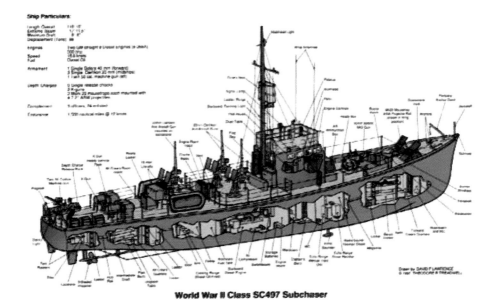

World War II Class SC497 Subchaser

Color Plates 5 and 6

U.S.O. TUNIS, N.W. AFRICA 1943
by
Watercolor, George Amaral

Color Plates 7 and 8

Color Plates 9 and 10

Color Plate 11

Color Plate 12

Color Plate 13

Color Plate 14

Color Plate 15

Color Plate 16

'Signet'
Created by:

Bill Tormey
EM1/c, USN

U.S.S PC 1178

Color Plates 17 and 18

©WALT DISNEY

Color Plates 19 and 20

Color Plates 21 and 22

AUGIE
USS INAUGURAL
AM 242

Color Plates 23 and 24

Color Plates 25 and 26

NOTES

1. The Coast Guard is now in the Department of Homeland Security. Page 10.

2. Boot Camp was the name given to the Navy Training Stations where recruits received their indoctrination into the Navy and learned the elements of seamanship, gunnery, and other naval skills. Page 11.

3. Most ships had small lockers aboard where each man could store his possessions. Men often stored their empty Sea Bags flattened under their mattresses. Hammocks were frequently commandeered by the ship to be used for damage control if needed. Page 12.

4. See Appendix C for complements of the ships. Page 12.

5. The name and symbol were not official, and their use was and is not an infringement on the Walt Disney character. Page 20.

6. For a discussion of SCTC see the book by Wm. J. Veigele titled *PC Patrol Craft of World War II* in the Bibliography. Page 21.

7. Because the Coast Guard was under the Navy during the war references in this book to Navy imply also the Coast Guard. Page 32.

8. Until about mid-1943 the Navy did not have a Third Class Petty Officer rate for engineers. The equivalent rate was Fireman 1/C. The next step up was Petty Officer 2/C. Page 35.

9. See the <u>Submarine Chaser Manual</u> in the Bibliography. This manual was a "Restricted Document" issued only to officers at SCTC. Page 38.

10. See the picture of a sailor shouldering his Sea Bag in Figure 4 of Appendix A. Page 48.

11. A heaving line was a line like a clothes line, one end of which could be thrown to handlers on a dock. The other end was tied to a ship's mooring line that was pulled to the dock by the handlers. Page 49.

12. CAT was an abbreviation for catarrh, an inflamation of a mucous membrane. Page 52.

13. Engineers wore their rates on the left sleeves of their uniforms, and deck rates wore theirs on their right sleeves. Page 75.

14. Corvettes were some of the first, but they were larger ships. Converted yachts also were used. Soon after the PCs, the SC subchasers joined the battle. Page 78.

15. For a list of all PCs transferred during and after the war see the book by Wm. J. Veigele in the Bibliography. Page 79.

16. For details see the book by Veigele in the Bibliography. Page 97.

162.17. For an account of the SCs of World War II see Treadwell, Theodore R., *Splinter Fleet – The Wooden Subchasers of World War II* listed in the Bibliography. Page 98.

18. See the book by Theodore Treadwell in the Bibliography. Page 108.

19. Yoke, Mike, and Sugar were the phonetic letters of the alphabet for YMS. Page 118.

20. In recent years the Coast Guard was in the Department of Transportation. It now is part of the Department of Homeland Security. Page 119.

21. The Coast Guard also manned 75 Frigates (PF). Page 119.

22. *Black Tie* takes charter cruises and offers Bed and Breakfast on the Caloosahatchee River in Florida. A number of ex-SCs are still active today in various capacities. They are discussed in the book *Splinter Fleet* by Theodore Treadwell listed in the Bibliography. Page 154.

23. Larger and more detailed plans for the ships here and also the ship types LSM, LSD, LCT, LCS, LCI, YTB, YTL, ATF, ASR, MP, DE, DD, CVE, and CVN are available from John Tombaugh 5009 West Beaman Lane, Rochester, Indiana 46975. Page 156.

24. During WWII the U. S. sent 45 PCs to other countries, 33 to France. After the war 110 were transferred to other countries, 4 to France. Page

25. For a brief summary of the history of PC 1120 see the book *PC Patrol Craft of World War II* listed in the Bibliography. Page 166.

26. The museum is in the Bay County Historical Society Museum located at 321 Washington Avenue, Bay City, Michigan 48708. Page 189.

27. In 1945 the Navy abandoned the use of hammocks which became government property. On 15 October of that year the Navy declared mattresses government property. Sailors no longer toted hammocks and mattresses. The Navy supplied them at stations and on ships, but the men kept their mattress covers. Page 217.

INDEX